A gift for

_____

From

_____

On this date

_____

This is normally where you would find lots of flashy endorsements from flashy celebrities. But since I'm a real, imperfect, as-far-from-flashy-as-it-gets woman and I write real and imperfect stories for real and imperfect women (and men!), this time around I wanted to do things a little differently. This time, I wanted YOU, my readers, my real and imperfect and beautiful readers, to be the ones to tell other real and imperfect and beautiful people what you loved about this book. So for you there, yes, you, holding this book in your hands, wondering if you should buy it, here's what women and men just like you had to say about it:

Truthful, insightful, and inspiring! *Beautiful Uncertainty* is a celebration of God's grace, peace, and love for all of us.

—Jodi Massengale, fabulous 40-something in California

Honest, down-to-earth, soul-bearing. *Beautiful Uncertainty* has become my personal reminder that there is at least one person out there among the 7 billion who gets it and also that there is One being in the universe (God) who is dying for me to allow Him to walk with me on this journey.

—Kirabo Byabashaija, incredibly shy almost-30 adventurer, in Uganda

Mandy is ingenuously candid in *Beautiful Uncertainty* regarding her struggles, her journey, and her passionate love for Christ. One thing is for certain in this *Beautiful Uncertainty*: Mandy has an inspiring way of reminding us that we are at no time, ever, alone.

—BECKY WILKENSON, 80S BIG-HAIR SURVIVOR, SINGLE
MOM OF TWO TEENS, SCHOOL COUNSELOR, IN ALABAMA

Beautiful Uncertainty is an incredible read. Mandy does such an amazing job reminding us that even when our lives feel chaotic, we live for a God who is unwavering.

—TORI FIORENZA, FORMER REALITY TV COMPETITOR ON
MTV'S *THE CHALLENGE* AND MOM OF TWO IN CHICAGO

I identified so much with Mandy's words, and I felt myself becoming stronger with each chapter of *Beautiful Uncertainty*. Mandy's strong sense of faith really shines through and will be an inspiration to anyone who reads this book.

—ALLISON ACQUAVIVA, 22-YEAR-OLD ANIMAL ADVOCATE
AND FAITHFUL FOLLOWER OF CHRIST, IN NEW YORK

Beautiful Uncertainty explores unchanging truths and challenges your faith to run wild. This book strengthened my faith while challenging me to embrace God's moments of silence and enjoy the journey!

—CHRIS OSMORE, UNCONVENTIONAL COFFEE DRINKER,
VIDEO PRODUCER, AND FAN OF GIRAFFES, IN ALABAMA

I love this book! Reading it is like sitting down with your best friend and talking about life.

—Carla Patton, Former CSI agent and lover of
cats, chocolate, coffee, and God, in Kansas

Beautiful Uncertainty is so beautifully written. It gave me so much hope for the future by reminding me to enjoy the process of being single because God is always in control.

—Camille Salazar, 20-something gal with a wild
heart and a happy gypsy soul, in the Philippines

Mandy courageously shares her story to encourage us not only as single women—but as *women*—to live boldly, trusting in God's beautiful timing.

—Nightingale Ngo, pianist, organist, musicologist,
and teacher, in Miami

Beautiful Uncertainty captures much about my past stagnant love life, my eager desire to serve others, and my desperation to know Christ more. I know there are women who need to hear its message today.

—Akirah Robinson, creator of akirahrobinson.com,
writer, therapist, and wife, in Pittsburgh

If you're struggling with the waiting, the not knowing, the heartache, or just want to know Jesus more, this book has it all.

—Megan Matheny, single lover and pursuer of Jesus,
race car driver, and music enthusiast, in Orlando

Mandy Hale does it again! She captures every thought I've had when it comes to being a single woman! It is clear in *Beautiful Uncertainty* that God always has a hand in things.

—Ruby Rodriguez, 36-year-old who still believes in happily ever after, in San Antonio

In her new book *Beautiful Uncertainty*, Mandy does not disappoint. Mandy gives a brand-new perspective on being single. This book brought me even closer to God and taught me that it is okay to be a single 37-year-old woman.

—Jenny Woods, trusting my struggles, in Virginia Beach, Virginia

Beautiful Uncertainty, unlike any self-improvement book on the market, provides hope for a generation of women who can find true fulfillment in a season often marred by brokenness and dark and doubt-filled places by turning their hearts and their attention to the one relationship that has absolute and beautiful certainty, the one shared with Jesus Christ.

—Bree Blum, single, 30-something creator of The Imperfect Vessel who loves Jesus, in West Virginia

I don't think I've ever come across a story more profound than Mandy's. *Beautiful Uncertainty* has raised the bar. Single women the world over will find this book enchanting!

—Joanne Oji, lawyer and reader who reads everything (including bus tickets), in Nigeria

This book is very adventurous, witty, and has lots of great insight! Mandy is such a great storyteller. I kept noticing myself wanting to dig right into the next chapter. Excellent read . . . even for men!

—Derek Evans, owner of Project 615, in Nashville

A very brave and vulnerable retelling of a significant year in Mandy's womanhood and career. Thoughtful, funny, and charming prose for women of faith trying to work out their process of "becoming" in the world.

—S. C. Lourie, magic-in-the-messy mama-writer and creator of *Butterflies & Pebbles*, in London

Beautiful Uncertainty will challenge you in the most beautiful ways possible, and if you allow, it will be just the inspiration you need to change your life and deepen your relationship with Jesus.

—Ashleydawn Wells, spokeswoman for InnerBeauty and southerner in love with Jesus, in Florida

Beautiful Uncertainty is the book that every woman needs in her life. This is by far Mandy's most vulnerable, uplifting, and inspiring book yet. Mandy captures the true trenches and peaks in life that women face in today's world. *Beautiful Uncertainty* is beautifully written, incredibly encouraging, and a forever favorite.

—Jordan Marie Davis, Miss Tennessee USA 2014, author of *Letters to my Beloved*, in Nashville

Mandy is blessed with a special way of presenting a sensible approach to handling seasons of uncertainty with humor, grace, and understanding of self through the Word of God. Each section of *Beautiful Uncertainty* encourages readers to have faith in God's perfect plan for their life.

—Reena Patton, single, Christian, and beautifully uncertain, in Los Angeles

Mandy Hale has awakened my soul and changed my life. I am a much happier and more spiritual person because of her words. *Beautiful Uncertainty* had me laughing, crying, smiling, and wanting more.

—Christine Darnell, blessed and loving New Yorker

In *Beautiful Uncertainty*, Mandy reminds me that life is a roller coaster no matter what our age, but God has us through all of the twists and turns!

—Jordan Deshler, bubbly bookworm and future world-changer, in Nashville

While reading *Beautiful Uncertainty*, I literally laughed out loud on one page and then had tears streaming down my face while reading the next page. For the first time in a long time, I'm excited about the future, and I'm now learning to live with my own beautiful uncertainty.

—Lori Diaz, 30-ish entrepreneur, owner of The Faded Farmhouse, and newly single mom, in Nashville

Mandy has done a masterful job with *Beautiful Uncertainty*. I love her honesty about what truly happens when we let go and fall in love with Jesus.

RUBY GETTINGER, STAR OF THE EMMY-NOMINATED *RUBY*, GRACIE AWARD WINNER, AUTHOR, IN GEORGIA

Through *Beautiful Uncertainty*, Mandy has given us another tool to navigate the world of single life. Thanks to her, my dry-erase board is full of the best inspirational quotes!

—SHACURAH HARDY, 20-SOMETHING, GOD-FEARING, AVID READER, IN RICHMOND, VIRGINIA

Too often during hardships we turn away from God, but with books like *Beautiful Uncertainty*, Mandy reminds us to keep Him in the driver's seat. It will allow you to see how much God really loves you.

—MARIANNE JORDAN, CREATOR OF MYOWNDIVA.COM, IN COLUMBUS, GEORGIA

This book is a beautiful reminder that God is the author of my life and that He has the perfect story already written for me. *Beautiful Uncertainty* reminded me that God is with me each step of the way, and He has already made my crooked paths straight.

—STEPHANIE NALBANDIAN, BELIEVER IN GOD'S PROMISES, IN KENNESAW, GEORGIA

Honesty, inspiration, humor, closure, and hope await you in *Beautiful Uncertainty*.

—TERA LEE FLAMAN, SASSY CANADIAN, IN CENTRAL ALBERTA

Mandy Hale is like a soul whisperer in *Beautiful Uncertainty*. It was like she was reading my mind! She helped me translate thoughts I didn't even know I had through this book.

—JESSICA NORTHEY, SOCIAL MEDIA MAVERICK AND
CREATOR OF *CM CHAT* AND *HEYSTAR!*, IN PHOENIX

In *Beautiful Uncertainty*, Mandy Hale invites us on a personal journey filled with twists and turns, surprises, heartache, frustrations, and incredible joy. She's embracing becoming the woman God made her to be with every fiber in her being; she's embracing the beautiful uncertainty of not knowing what's next and being okay with that; and she's inviting us to do the same.

—EMILY CUMMINS, PASTOR'S KID, CREATOR OF
WWW.BECOMINGME.TV

MANDY HALE

THOMAS NELSON

Since 1798

Published in Nashville, Tennessee, by Thomas Nelson. Thomas Nelson is a registered trademark of HarperCollins Christian Publishing, Inc.

Thomas Nelson titles may be purchased in bulk for educational, business, fund-raising, or sales promotional use. For information, please e-mail SpecialMarkets@ThomasNelson.com.

Quote on page 183 is taken from *Arms Wide Open* by Sherri Gragg © 2014 by Sherri Gragg. Used by permission of Thomas Nelson. www.thomasnelson.com

Scripture quotations marked ESV are taken from the ESV® Bible (The Holy Bible, English Standard Version®). Copyright © 2001 by Crossway, a publishing ministry of Good News Publishers. Used by permission. All rights reserved. Scripture quotations marked THE MESSAGE are taken from *The Message*. Copyright © by Eugene H. Peterson 1993, 1994, 1995, 1996, 2000, 2001, 2002. Used by permission of Tyndale House Publishers, Inc. Scripture qutotations marked NASB are taken from the New American Standard Bible®. Copyright © 1960, 1962, 1963, 1968, 1971, 1972, 1973, 1975, 1977, 1995 by The Lockman Foundation. Used by permission. (www. Lockman.org). Scripture quotations marked NIV are taken from the the Holy Bible, New International Version®, NIV®. Copyright © 1973, 1978, 1984, 2011 by Biblica, Inc.® Used by permission of Zondervan. All rights reserved worldwide. www.zondervan.com. *The "NIV" and "New International Version" are trademarks registered in the United States Patent and Trademark Office by Biblica, Inc.*® Scripture quotations marked NKJV are taken from the New King James Version®. © 1982 by Thomas Nelson. Used by permission. All rights reserved. Scripture quotations marked NLT are taken from the Holy Bible, New Living Translation. © 1996, 2004, 2007, 2013 by Tindale House Foundation. Used by permission of Tyndale House Publishers, Inc., Carol Stream, Illinois 60188. All rights reserved.

ISBN-13: 978-0-7180-7608-5

Printed in the United States

15 16 17 18 19 QG 5 4 3 2 1

To my readers:
Thank you for taking this beautifully
uncertain journey with me.
Being a part of your lives has been one
of the biggest blessings of mine.
This one's for you.

Contents

CONTENTS

Introduction

There's a lot of uncertainty about single life. Uncertainty about whom to date. Whom to love. Who loves you back. Where to work. Sometimes how to pay the next bill. How to cook. Should you venture out to that movie or restaurant alone or wait for a friend to join you? Should you buy a house or keep renting? Try online dating or play it safe? (And then sometimes you venture onto an online dating site briefly, only to get hit on by a man three times your age who is proudly posing with his prized stuffed turkey in his profile pic, and you dart quickly back to the certain path of safety. This is a strictly hypothetical scenario, of course.)

Every single day reminds me of the many, many uncertainties of single life . . . and how those same uncertainties brought me here, to this place, as a writer. As a blogger. As an author. As someone you have invited into your world, at least for a little while, by reading these words.

Just six short years ago, I was trapped in a toxic,

abusive relationship that would ultimately change everything about my life; I just didn't know it at the time. Night after night after night you could find me hidden away in my bedroom in the apartment I shared with my agnostic boyfriend, crying out helplessly to God from one of the darkest corners I'd ever found myself cowering in. God's grace is big enough to cover sinful decisions, as it turns out. And it was during that time when I first began to really experience and embrace the beautiful uncertainty of not just believing in God, but of walking with Him. I knew without a doubt God was going to deliver me from that relationship; I just didn't know how. And at that moment, I didn't need to know how. I just needed to draw near to Him and trust Him.

I became a Christian at age twenty. But I don't feel that I truly became a Christ follower until those nights of helplessness spent on my knees before Him six years ago. It took fleeing from an unhealthy relationship to send me running straight into His arms. I didn't have a close relationship with Jesus until that season of surrendered uncertainty made Him come alive to me in a whole new way. I knew *of* Him, but I didn't *know* Him. I talked *at* Him, but I didn't listen *to* Him. My heart was in the right place, and I loved Him, but I didn't seek after Him. I didn't pursue a relationship with Him. I didn't really listen to Him much at all actually. It must have made Him really sad.

But you know what? He was faithful, even if I wasn't. If you've read my other books, you know what happened next. A few weeks later I was free of that relationship and setting the only New Year's resolution I have ever kept: to write more and to find a way to inspire others with my story.

God met me there—right in the middle of my hopelessness, sinfulness, and powerlessness—and He turned my life around. He became *real* to me. He didn't wait until I'd cleaned myself up to intervene. He didn't reprimand me before He redeemed me. And He also didn't hand me a roadmap before we started our journey together. He simply stepped in, took the controls, and started to rebuild my life one brick and one miracle at a time, always calling me to greater levels of trust and faith and boldness. Not because I had all the answers, but because I had finally surrendered to the One who did.

Over the next five years, He would continue to guide me and prune me and use me, never failing to blow my mind as I watched Him work in and through my life to impact the lives of others. (Like you, there, holding this book.) Through my own trial and error, hijinks, heartbreaks, stubbornness, sinfulness, and humanness, He managed to do what I asked Him to do—make my story count—over and over and over again, sometimes in the most unbelievable, jaw-dropping, and, yes, even hilarious ways. (My walk with Him is anything but orthodox.) And the uncertainty I once ran from in my life—from being a planner and a controller and a completely neurotic, type A personality—I began to embrace in my life. The uncertainty of singleness. The uncertainty of completely surrendering to Him, no matter what. The uncertainty of stepping out in faith, even when fear and the certainty of playing it safe fought to hold me back.

The *beautiful uncertainty*.

Then a little more than a year ago, I said a prayer that changed my walk with Him yet again.

When I set my goals for 2014 and created my yearly vision board (you'll find instructions for creating your own board later in the book), I listed only one goal for the year. One goal. No other dreams or plans or hopes for my career or love life. What was that one goal?

I will seek, pursue, and fall in love with Jesus with radical abandon.

(Warning: *only* say this prayer if you're prepared for your entire world to be rocked on its very axis.)

Over the next year, I would see miracles abound: From the planning and implementation of a nationwide book and speaking tour in only a little more than a month, to the removal of a relationship that had left me in limbo for seven long years. From standing on a stage with my knees knocking in front of twenty thousand women at one of my biggest hero's conferences to finally finding the physical home where my soul belonged in the form of a beautiful ranch in the country.

I DISCOVERED THE BEAUTIFUL TRUTH THAT WHEN YOU SEEK FIRST THE KINGDOM OF GOD AND HIS RIGHTEOUSNESS, ALL THINGS REALLY ARE ADDED TO YOU.

And, in my journey at least, I found that when you seek Him first, the things that aren't part of His plan are taken away.

So now I want to invite you to travel with me through that wonderful, painful, magical, challenging, life-altering year of highs and lows, tragedies and triumphs, snowstorms and earthquakes, high stakes and heartbreaks, great wins and great losses, and shedding tears and overcoming fears. On the pages that follow, you'll find essays, prayers, lessons, inspiration, and hopefully a little encouragement. You might even get so lost that you find yourself. And most of all, you'll find beautiful uncertainty. You may not find all the answers, but I hope when you're finished reading, you'll feel brave enough to start asking the questions—of yourself and of God (even the really hard ones).

Whether you're idling in stubborn sinfulness or

walking in seemingly never-ending singleness or living with any sort of uncertainty—waiting for love, waiting for marriage, waiting for babies, waiting for a cure, or a miracle, or a sign, or for God—I hope my journey will help make the wait a little easier and the uncertainty a little bit more beautiful.

My walk with Him has not, is not, and will never be perfect, but it is *real*. It's real and raw and messy, unclear and doubt-filled and, at times, rebellious. As I'm sure yours is. But it's the most beautiful walk I've ever taken. Because the destination doesn't matter. Holding His hand for the journey is enough.

He's always just enough light for the step I'm on. And His presence is always a beautiful certainty, even when absolutely nothing else is.

Prayer

God help me to see the good in the "not knowing" . . . the joy in the "in-between" . . . the meaning in the "meantime."

PART ONE

Winter

A Date with God

A couple of years ago a friend told me about a season she had right before she got married when she decided to spend six months "dating" Jesus. She told me she would fix Him a cup of coffee in the mornings and even reach over and buckle His seat belt when she would be driving somewhere. Her goal was to focus all of her time and energy on Him the way she had focused it on so many fruitless relationships over the years. It sounded incredibly intriguing (and also a little weird), but as I listened, all I could picture was me sitting in Starbucks talking to God in an empty chair across from me and being carted off the premises in a straitjacket.

Before I made a snap judgment about her sanity (or mine), however, I decided that—like a lot of things in life—you shouldn't knock it until you've tried it. I mean, if Jesus is alive and present and on the move in our day-to-day lives thanks to the Holy Spirit (which He is), who's to say my friend hadn't stumbled onto a really genius concept?

A few days later I was in line at Zaxby's waiting to

order lunch when I felt God begin to tug at my heart. *"Order something for Me too,"* I could feel Him whisper into my spirit. (And when I talk about God speaking to me, I should clarify that I've never heard an audible voice.)

HE LAYS THINGS ON MY HEART IN SUCH A POWERFUL WAY, I KNOW IT'S HIM NUDGING ME OR LEADING ME TO DO SOMETHING.

When I felt His gentle tug, I immediately started to argue with Him. "But, God, Zaxby's is a little pricey. You want me to order a full meal for You that's just going to sit there and go to waste?"

As soon as I responded to God with those words, I could just imagine him laughing at me. (Yes, sometimes I wonder if God is chuckling at my shenanigans. Often, actually. I think He must get such a kick out of me and my ridiculousness.)

"Mandy. I give you breath and life and a heartbeat every single day, *and you can't spare seven dollars for Me?"*

So I ordered God a chicken finger plate with extra Zax sauce, just like me. (I figured God surely loved Zax sauce since it *has* to be the modern-day equivalent of manna from heaven.) And when I got home, I sat down at my desk with both our meals and started to eat. Now obviously God didn't beam down from heaven and join me for chicken tenders. But what followed was the sweetest thirty to forty-five minutes of communion with Him I had ever had. There was something so moving about sitting at my desk that day, quietly sharing a meal with the God of the universe. There was something even more moving about the fact that *He* wanted to share a meal with *me*. Me. Little ol' me. Imperfect, greatly flawed, often the conductor of the Hot Mess Express *me*. And yet, there He was, standing at the door of my heart knocking, waiting to come in and eat with me (Revelation 3:20).

I had gone into this experiment with no small amount of uncertainty, even a little hesitation, wondering if my simple offering was silly or pointless or even crazy, but I ended up eating my chicken tenders with tears rolling down my face and His presence hovering all around me.

THAT'S THE GOD WE SERVE. A DEEPLY PERSONAL GOD WHO WANTS TO BE A PART OF OUR MOST ORDINARY MOMENTS. IN THE BEAUTIFUL UNCERTAINTY OF OUR EVERYDAY LIVES, HE LONGS TO BE OUR MOST BEAUTIFUL CONSTANT.

Later, of course, I ended up eating the second meal myself. And I never regretted the seven-dollar investment, not even for a moment. Because I consider that day my first real "date" with God.

It was the best seven dollars I'd ever spent.

BEAUTIFUL CERTAINTY:

As much of a mess as I can be, and as flawed as I am, I can honestly say my relationship with Jesus never fails to bring me great surprise and laughter and joy. If you don't have that kind of relationship with Him, it is my hope that this story (and this book) will inspire you. So much of the beauty, heart, and messy realness of Christianity is lost in our attempts to be perfect and to convince other people we are. And so many precious moments of closeness and intimacy with God are lost in our fear of being judged, or looking silly, or being afraid to approach Him as a *friend*. Just stop. Get real. Be who you are with Him, warts and all.

JESUS WON'T RUN FROM YOUR WEAKNESS, YOUR HUMANNESS. HE'LL RUN TO IT.

He'll honor your willingness to seek Him above all else. And along the way, the two of you might even share a few laughs.

Prayer

God, thank You that with You, even the most ordinary moments can be extraordinarily beautiful. Help me to come to know You, not just as a Father and as a Savior but as a Friend.

One Year, One Goal

*B*efore each new year begins, I usually fill a vision board with at least twenty to twenty-five goals and resolutions for the next twelve months. And over the past several years, I've seen amazing things happen and dreams realized that were lifted verbatim off my simple little dry-erase board.

On the cusp of 2014, however, I wanted to do things a little differently. I listed only one goal on my vision board for the *entire year*:

> I will seek, pursue, and fall in love with Jesus with radical abandon.

After writing that resolution on my vision board in late 2013, my life seemed to kick into overdrive. It was as though the shift in my priorities had shifted me to the next level! Things with my career were booming. The website and my social media platforms were thriving. My friendships were being strengthened. I even started getting healthier in my eating and exercise habits.

Most importantly, my relationship with Jesus did indeed become the most precious, life-giving, and joy-producing relationship of all. I was taking time to meditate and be still and get silent and stop talking *at* Him and instead listen *to* Him. My life had never felt more hopeful and exciting, and, well . . . *alive.*

> "Seek first the kingdom of God and his righteousness, and all these things will be added to you."
> —Matthew 6:33 ESV

It's like God wanted me to see, really *see*, that I never had to seek success at all. Or friendships. Or love. Or opportunity. Or anything other than Him. We hear the Scriptures and we learn the Scriptures and we recite the Scriptures, but when we actually *see* the Scriptures lift right off the page and play out in real time, in real ways in our lives . . . it's awe inspiring.

And the best part was, I didn't *want* to pursue anything other than Him. The more He added to my life, the less I needed anything other than Him. It was the most perfect example of the upside-down way Jesus does things in His kingdom. The last will become first, the humble will be exalted, the poor will become rich. The more I had of Him, the less I needed anything else.

Turns out, the more you seek Him and the more you

find Him, the less you need the "things." He is beautifully, perfectly, entirely *enough*.

EXERCISE: CREATE YOUR OWN VISION BOARD

Creating your own vision board is super easy to do, and the benefits far outweigh the cost! There's something powerful about writing out your prayers and dreams and goals and having them posted somewhere where you see them every single day. Plus, it's biblical: "Where there is no vision, the people perish" (Proverbs 29:18 KJV).

I created my vision board from a plain white dry-erase board. It's as easy breezy as that. Most of the time I simply write my goals, dreams, prayers, and plans in list format, but occasionally I will tape some pictures up for added encouragement. You could also use a bulletin board if you prefer to have nothing but pictures for inspiration. Obviously, Pinterest makes for an excellent and endless source of material—from pictures to healthy eating plans to quotes and everything else in between!

Before you begin your board, I would encourage you to say a prayer and ask God to reveal what He would have you focus on for the weeks, months, or even year ahead. Had I not done that, I wouldn't have been led to write only one goal on my vision board for 2014, and the incredible year that followed might have never happened, including the inspiration for this book!

You can change your list as often as you want— or as quickly as you start checking off goals. You'll be surprised to see how being bold enough to lay out your dreams in black and white has a way of bringing them to life. And most importantly, hang your board in a place where you will see it at least a couple of times a day. I try to read through mine every morning when I wake up and at night before I go to sleep.

You don't have to wait for a new year, a new month, a new week, or even a new day to create your vision board. You can start now!

Happy dreaming, praying, envisioning, pinning, creating, and realizing!

Coffee with Jesus

*A*s 2013 was drawing to a close, God had begun to shake my spiritual foundations to the core. I suspect so He could put down new ones.

I had my one goal in place for the upcoming year and was attending a new Bible study that had revolutionized my relationship with Jesus. One night a wonderful lady stood up and gave her testimony about her quiet time with the Lord, and her words left me speechless. When she enters into her quiet time, she sits in her favorite place and visualizes she's there with Jesus, simply having a conversation with Him. Her place is her front-porch swing, but you can really pick any place that represents peace and calm and openness to you. (You can actually do this wherever you are, even if you are on the other side of the world from your special place. Just close your eyes and picture yourself there! That's the beauty of meditation.)

Why had I never thought of this before? Why had I just always talked *at* Him and not *to* Him?

In case the concept of spending quiet time with God is unfamiliar to you (as it was to me for a long time), it's basically taking time either within your normal prayer time or throughout the day to get silent before God and listen for His voice. The Bible tells us in John 16:13: "But when He, the Spirit of truth, comes, He will guide you into all the truth; for He will not speak on His own initiative, but whatever He hears, He will speak; and He will disclose to you what is to come" (NASB).

THE HOLY SPIRIT WANTS TO TALK TO US. BUT HE IS A GENTLEMAN. HE WILL NOT ATTEMPT TO COMPETE WITH THE NOISE AROUND US, OR SHOUT TO BE HEARD OVER NETFLIX, OR FORCE US TO LISTEN AT ALL, IF WE ARE DETERMINED NOT TO.

Think about it. If you had a friend who was always talking, talking, talking but never stopped to take a breath and listen to what you had to say, would the friendship last very long? Our relationship with God is much the same way. It can be either as shallow as we settle for or as deep as we are willing to go.

Well, I decided I was tired of the kiddie pool. I wanted to go deeper with Him. I wanted to know Him more.

I wanted to know Him all I could.

The place where I began to visualize myself talking to Jesus was in front of my fireplace with a cup of coffee. And that is where my quiet time is spent to this day. Warmth to me fosters communion and closeness and conversation. I sit by my little fireplace with my cup of coffee and picture Him there with me and invite Him to join me in my quiet time and tell me anything He wants me to know. Most days don't start until I've had my fireside chat with Jesus. My prayer time has never been so rich or so sweet. We don't hurry, Jesus and me. We take our time. Sometimes I talk first; sometimes I simply wait. It's becoming easier and easier to close my eyes and see Him sitting there beside me, coffee mug in hand.

Sometimes He speaks to my spirit. Sometimes we sit silently. I tell Him funny things. I tell Him serious things. I ask Him questions. Sometimes He answers. Sometimes He doesn't. Sometimes I picture us toasting our coffee mugs together in celebration when something really good happens.

But whatever we do, it's beautiful. It's beautiful and uncertain and even a little vulnerable, inviting Jesus to join me in the midst of whatever mess I've created this week. It's all about patience and childlike faith and a willingness to wait.

As are most worthwhile endeavors in life.

BEAUTIFUL CERTAINTY:

I'm learning God wants to speak to us, and we have to offer Him the beautiful silence to do so. When I quiet my heart and my thoughts and just draw close to Him, I begin to hear His still, small voice in my spirit. Today I urge you to stop talking and stop asking and stop begging and stop requesting and just get silent in His presence and *listen*. Who knows? His still, small voice might just blow your mind.

Prayer

God, thank You for the sweetness of Your presence. Show me how to not just talk *at* You but to listen *to* You. Remove any distraction that would keep me from hearing Your still, small voice.

If an Ex Pokes You on Facebook and You Don't Respond, Did Anything Actually Happen?

***

Even though I hesitate to give him one more keystroke or one more dot of ink on the pages of my life, the continuing saga of Mr. E and me (my on-again/off-again ex of seven years) is a story that needs to be told. Because, you see, the story finally gets a conclusion this time.

He came back into my life on a Monday.

As you may recall, at the end of *I've Never Been to Vegas but My Luggage Has*, I hadn't spoken to Mr. E in six months. That six months stretched into a year, and then almost another year until the final weeks of 2013, when I suddenly found myself Facebook to Facebook with Mr. E.

Being that it had been one year, ten months, and eighteen days since we had spoken a word to one another, and given his penchant for grand gestures, you're probably thinking he swept back into my life with great pomp and circumstance, right?

Yeah. No. It was in the form of (drumroll, please) . . .

A Facebook poke.

Are you kidding me?

Let me take a moment to say here and now that I have never understood Facebook pokes. They are weird. They seem antiquated, like something better suited for Myspace. And they're completely arbitrary and random. What does a "poke" mean, exactly? That you want to talk? Then why not just send me a message? Call me crazy, but I just think there are a lot better ways to communicate than through a Facebook poke.

But I digress. Then again, this was Mr. E. He wasn't exactly known for his communication skills.

Why now? Why after almost two years was this epic character from my past choosing to reemerge into my present?

And what was I supposed to do about it? Ignore him? Or, dare I . . . poke back?

I remember asking my Twitter friends what it all meant. I actually tweeted, "If an ex pokes you on Facebook and you don't respond, did anything actually happen?" After much debate, the general consensus seemed to be that Facebook poking was sometimes a way for someone you hadn't spoken to in a while to reestablish communication. A safety net, in a manner of speaking. Reaching out and indicating interest in talking without putting much on the line (well, that part sounded familiar). So there it was. This was clearly Mr. E's way of letting me know he was back on the grid of my life, if I wanted him there.

But did I want him there? That was the real question. Perhaps my reaction to the poke was less confusion about what a Facebook poke meant and more about what a Facebook poke from Mr. E meant.

God had let me know me almost two years prior, after the last time I spoke with Mr. E, that I was not to contact him anymore until He freed me to do so. That I was to completely walk away and let him go and do nothing whatsoever except pray for him. That was the only action I felt freed to take on behalf of this giant question mark of a relationship.

So I did. Night after night, for almost two years, I prayed for him. From the darkness of my front steps on cold winter nights. From beneath the shade of my favorite tree at the park on warm spring days. From my table at Starbucks watching the brilliantly hued autumn leaves drift slowly to the ground on crisp fall afternoons. For two years I cried out to God on Mr. E's behalf. In the silence, in the quiet, it seemed absolutely nothing was happening on the surface to move either God *or* Mr. E to make any sort of a bold move on behalf of our relationship. I couldn't see any sign that anything in the heavens or on the earth was being shaken. (But the beautiful thing about God is that in the middle of the uncertainty of my relationship with Mr. E, I was being drawn closer to Him.)

And then came the infamous Facebook poke. It was so ridiculous and so hilarious and yet, at the same time, so wildly appropriate that our paths would converge again . . . on social media. (Hadn't God made really big moves in my life over the past few years via social media?)

Taking that into consideration, remembering all the prayers on all the nights over the past two years of silence, and remembering the five years of history prior to that, I took a deep breath . . .

And I poked him back.

My seven years of back and forth with Mr. E had been sometimes beautiful, mostly uncertain. (As matters of the heart often are.) Maybe he didn't deserve another chance. Or even a Facebook poke. But I knew whatever happened, God had my back.

WHEN YOU KNOW GOD IS YOUR SAFETY NET, SUDDENLY LEAPS OF FAITH DON'T LOOK SO SCARY.

BEAUTIFUL CERTAINTY:

As scary as it might be to take a chance . . . it's scarier not to. There comes a time when you have to just stop waiting for the answers and start boldly living with the questions. As for me? I pray I'm always brave enough to take the shot. Go for it. Leap without looking. And walk through fear to see what—and who—is on the other side.

IF YOU TRUST GOD AND TAKE A CHANCE, GOOD THINGS MIGHT HAPPEN OR BAD THINGS MIGHT HAPPEN. BUT IF YOU DON'T TAKE A CHANCE, NOTHING HAPPENS.

Prayer

God, thank You that when You are at the center of my life, I can take bold steps and chances and risks with confidence, knowing that even if things go wrong, You can find a way to turn it for my good.

Lessons Learned from a Homeless Man Named Louie

One afternoon as I was pulling out of McDonald's, iced coffee in hand, I spotted a homeless man standing on the side of the road, selling newspapers. This is a familiar sight in Nashville. Although I usually try to purchase the one-dollar newspapers when I see someone selling them, I didn't have cash, so I kept going. As I pulled out into the busy intersection to head to my meeting, however, the man waved at me, a sweet, humble smile on his face. Something about that wave and smile plucked at my heartstrings. I ignored it, though, wanting to get back on the road, since I knew there were still traffic jams to navigate. As I approached the red light to make a left turn and head back to the interstate, I felt God tugging at my heart.

"Mandy, turn around and go offer to buy that man something to eat."

I didn't hear the audible voice of God, but I knew in my heart what He was telling me to do.

Still, I tried to ignore it. I was running more than fifteen minutes late already.

"*Mandy.*" I felt God's insistent prodding. I continued to resist, arguing with Him in my mind.

"*God, I don't want to. I'm a single woman, alone, with no way to defend myself should he turn out to be dangerous. What if he's just a panhandler and not even really homeless? What if? What if, what if?*" You know, basically all the usual arguments we have with ourselves and with God to get out of confronting the problem of homelessness and poverty, and admitting maybe we can have a small hand in being the solution.

As the light turned green and I started to make the left turn that would take me back to the interstate and away from the man on the corner, something in me just couldn't turn my back on him. I swooped around in the middle of the road instead, making a U-turn and circling back around to him.

I rolled down my window, and the man approached me, somewhat shyly.

"Hello!" I greeted him. "I don't have any cash (which was true), but can I buy you something to eat or drink?"

He smiled. "Well, I sure do appreciate it, young lady. I'd love something to eat."

"What can I get for you?"

"Well," he looked a little bashful. His face was deeply tanned and lined with creases from long hours spent in the sun. He was clearly not impaired in any way, and although he was a bit rumpled and disheveled, he was dressed as nicely as one could be under his circumstances and seemed to take pride in his job selling newspapers. "It's fifty-cent cheeseburger day at McDonald's. How about four of those?"

The request broke my heart a little. I was offering to buy him anything he wanted to eat, and his biggest wish was four, fifty-cent cheeseburgers from McDonald's. That's all. He didn't even ask for a drink.

"Can't I get you something to wash them down with? A Coke, maybe?" I asked.

"Oh, no ma'am. The burgers will do just fine."

I assured him I'd be right back. And as I sat in the line at McDonald's, my eyes filled with tears. It would take me exactly five minutes and two dollars to make someone's day a little brighter, and I had almost passed up the opportunity to do so. Out of fear, out of doubt, out of my own selfish desires to get somewhere a little faster and avoid an inconvenience.

HOW OFTEN IN LIFE DO WE MISS OUT ON BLESSING SOMEONE BECAUSE WE DON'T WANT TO BE INCONVENIENCED?

When I got to the window, I was hit with sudden inspiration and ordered the four cheeseburgers . . . plus a large order of fries, two apple pies, and a large Coke. If I was going to be a blessing, I was going to be as big of a blessing as I could be—even if it was in the form of McDonald's. It's funny how God can use something as seemingly insignificant as a fifty-cent cheeseburger to love on one of His children.

The entire order was just seven dollars. (A fact not lost on me that my "meal with God" at Zaxby's a few weeks prior had been the same price.) Didn't Jesus say, "Whatever you did for one of the least of these brothers and sisters of mine, you did for me" (Matthew 25:40 NIV)?

I drove back to him and handed him the food. He took it from me gratefully. "God bless you, young lady."

"Can I ask you your name?" I asked him.

"Yes, ma'am. It's Louie." He handed me one of the wrinkled newspapers he had been clutching.

"Hi, Louie. I'm Mandy. Is there anything I can pray for you about?"

His kind, worn eyes crinkled at the sides when he smiled down at me.

"No, ma'am . . . but I'll be praying for you." Then he paused. "When you can't trace God's hand, you sure can trust His heart." He reached down and gave me a fist bump. I laughed.

"Thank you, Louie. I hope you have a great rest of the day."

"God bless you, Mandy." He trotted away clutching the drink and the bag of McDonald's goodies as if they were gold. And I headed back into traffic, my heart full.

Later I was reflecting on my encounter with this precious soul (that almost didn't happen) when God started to speak to me about several things. Things I can only hope I am able to do a good job of being a vessel and putting into words here.

1. How often do we ignore God's pullings and tuggings on our hearts because the thing He's telling us to do doesn't seem safe, or convenient, or sensible? We so often go through life looking for signs, angels, and touchstones to point us in the right direction but missing our opportunities to be those things for someone else. What if we're not always supposed to be on the lookout for our guardian angels? What if that's not enough? What if we're supposed to actually *be* those things for someone else?

2. When we do miss opportunities to be a blessing to others, we also lose the blessing ourselves. And I don't say that for ego-driven or pride-driven reasons. I'm sure Louie enjoyed his three-course meal from McDonald's, but there's no way he

enjoyed it even half as much as I enjoyed blessing him with it. It filled my heart with joy to fill that sweet man's belly with food, and it only cost me seven dollars. It often takes so little to bless someone so much. Why don't we do it more often?

3. This is the most important lesson I took from my encounter with Louie. He was homeless, disheveled, and likely not all that clean. Who knows how frequently he gets to bathe, living on the streets? His life in pieces all around him. His next meal, and even his next steps in life, uncertain. Yet, even in the midst of all that, and actually *because* of all that, he moved me. He captured my heart. I wanted to show him love. I wanted to do whatever I could to minister to him and bring him a little joy.

So what's my point in all this? We tend to run from God when we sin. We hide from Him when we mess up. We stand cowering in the corner of the ruins of our lives, scared to approach Him or face Him or ask Him for any kind of help because we're afraid He's mad at us. We're afraid we're too big of a mess for Him to possibly love us. We are pitifully human and entirely, and not always beautifully, uncertain. We are, in a sense, Louie.

But what if it's possible that if I, in all my fleshly, fallible, imperfect humanity, found something so sympathetic and so worthy of love in Louie, then maybe, just *maybe*, God isn't turned off or angry or unsympathetic with us in the middle of *our* messes? What if it is, in fact, exactly the opposite?

WHAT IF GOD SEES US STANDING THERE, HOPELESS AND HELPLESS AND ENSNARED IN THE CHAOS OF OUR OWN BAD CHOICES, AND INSTEAD OF TURNING HIS BACK ON US, IT MAKES HIM LONG TO OPEN HIS ARMS EVEN WIDER TO US?

What if we've been wrong about Him all along? What if He hates the sin because of what it's done to our lives but is still passionately in love with the sinner? What if He looks beyond the dirt and the muck and the filth and the garbage we've cluttered our lives with and sees only the beautiful, precious heart of His child beating underneath?

Or . . .

What if we're hanging our heads in shame, asking God for a fifty-cent cheeseburger because we don't feel like we're worthy of more than that, and all the while He longs to bless us with the burgers, the fries, the large Coke, and the apple pie?

BEAUTIFUL CERTAINTY:

I'm so thankful that despite what the world would have us believe, loving God isn't about being perfect or flawless or even having it all together. It's about loving God first, loving people second, and allowing God to use our imperfections, mistakes, and failures to glorify His strength, which is made perfect in our weakness (2 Corinthians 12:19). There is no one more usable to God than the imperfect person. And this is just one reason why I love Him so very much.

Prayer

God, help me to always seek to be a blessing to others, even when it's scary or uncertain or inconvenient ... especially then. May I never pass up an opportunity to allow Your love to shine through me. Help me learn to rest in Your grace even as I extend it to others, knowing there is nothing I can do to deserve it and also nothing I can do to cancel it out.

Clarity and Closure

After the Facebook poke between Mr. E and me, in the silence, in the moment between uncertainty and certainty when I battled between seeking clarity and seeking closure, I began to imagine what I would say to him after two years of silence.

Why was it so hard to figure out what I would say to him beyond a Facebook poke? For the same reason I tried to avoid all thoughts of Mr. E whenever possible: Because I wasn't over him. Because I still thought about him all the time. Because I had blocked his Facebook updates so they wouldn't come to my newsfeed because when and if the day came that something popped up telling me he was engaged or getting married or even just "in a relationship," I wasn't sure my heart would be able to handle it.

Had I put my life on hold for him? No. I lived fully and I lived big. And I tried to be as open as I possibly could to new love finding me. But at night, once I had taken off my makeup and my defenses were down and my mind started to wander, it seemed rather than new love sitting down at the table of my life to join me, old love managed to find its way back in . . . and I was back there again. Back in the middle of the moment when I last saw him, standing at a crowded train station in Queens, clinging to him for dear life, never wanting to let go . . . because I knew the moment I did, he would disappear down the street and out of my life with the same haste of a New York City taxi speeding away from the curb.

If I closed my eyes even a little, I was back in that moment, wondering what I could do or say differently to change the way the story went. To change the fact that more than two years would pass before I'd see him or talk to him, or even hear a word of any kind from him at all. I could still taste the tears and hear the sounds of the train speeding down the track. I could still smell his clean, fresh linen shirt as I rested my head on his shoulder for the last time. I could almost rewind every moment since that one and close my eyes tight enough to feel like, for a second, I was back there with him and we were still "us," and there was still a chance to find and mend the errant thread of our almost-relationship before it unraveled and left us spiraling off in separate directions, on separate coasts, living separate lives.

But I wasn't there. I couldn't change the story. I guess I wasn't meant to.

But if by some miracle or wrinkle in time or wiggle

of the nose or dash of fairy dust or clicking together of my heels three times, I could turn back the clock and go back to that moment, at that train station in Queens, here's what I would say:

> Did you ever really love me? Did you and I ever really become an "us" in your mind, or were we always "you" and "me"? Did you really plan on putting a ring on my finger? Was it all a mirage I saw because I wanted to see it and needed to see it, or did those moments that felt so magical to me happen for you too? Was I a "safe settle" or a conscious choice? If you knew in your heart this was the last time you'd see me . . . our last shot . . . would you do anything differently?

> And the questions that haunted me most of all . . .

> Did I imagine that this entire relationship meant more than it did? Was it all one-sided? Did I write and produce and star in a movie of my own making? Or were you in it with me, feeling and loving and trying and hurting and risking and soaring and losing and falling?
>
> Was I always your option . . . while you were my choice?

As much as I wanted clarity, as much I longed for answers, none were being given. At least not now.

And yet . . . yet . . . just giving myself permission to say things out loud, even to myself, that I had needed to say for so long brought me peace. And, dare I say it, closure?

I suppose part of getting the answers we seek is being bold enough to ask the questions and brave enough to face whatever is on the other side of those questions. Or maybe some answers simply aren't meant to be known because they would hurt too much. Or they would set us on a course where we don't belong. Or change our story altogether.

> MAYBE SOMETIMES THE NOT KNOWING IS BETTER THAN THE KNOWING—BECAUSE IN THE NOT KNOWING, WE CAN WRITE OUR OWN ENDING.

In the beautiful uncertainty of it all, we can find our own closure. Tell our own story, in the way we think it should be told. In the way we wished it would be told.

Or maybe it doesn't matter what questions we ask or don't ask or what things we say or don't say . . . because things are going to turn out the way they're going to turn out, regardless. Maybe no matter which way it would have gone that day, Mr. E and I still would have wound up as supporting actors in each other's stories rather than leads.

I don't know. And I can't go back in time, rewrite the past, or anything.

All I can do is hope that at future train stations, with future guys, at future times, the memory of not saying what I needed to say in the past would give me the courage to say everything I need to say in the present.

EXERCISE: A CLOSING CONVERSATION

Narrate a conversation between you and someone in your life whom you never had closure with (a friend, an ex, a family member, etc.). What would you say? What would they say? What outcome would you hope for?

_____

_____

_____

_____

_____

_____

_____

_____

_____

_____

_____

_____

_____

_____

_____

_____

_____

_____

_____

_____

_____

_____

_____

_____

Beautiful Uncertainty

The Year of Completion

I know you might want to throw this book against the wall right now, but bear with me. It's about to get good.

The Facebook poke led to a Facebook message, which led to an e-mail, which led to a phone call, which led to me waking up one morning to realize Mr. E was very much back in my life. But not so much in a romantic way. More like a friendship. A trusted, tried-and-true friendship. And it was different (I know I've said that every time, but this time it *was* different) because finally, *finally* my number-one priority had become seeking after Jesus and not seeking after Mr. E's love or attention or heart. I was a woman after God's heart, and that would set this chapter of Mr. E and me apart from any that had come before.

Even more interesting than anything happening between Mr. E and me was the fact that I had developed an intense desire to study the life of Jesus. I couldn't get enough of reading about Him: His life, His ministry,

His character. And it seemed everything I was reading and studying during that time frame kept pointing me, surprisingly, back to the Old Testament, to the book of Hosea. The book of Hosea has long been close to my heart because most Christians and biblical scholars agree it represents God's unfailing love, His unfailing grace, and His unfailing pursuit of His children.

I'm not going to get too deep into the theology here because I'm *not* a biblical scholar, but I would encourage you to do a separate study of the book of Hosea on your own. (The app *She Reads Truth* has an excellent one, and the book *Pursued* by Jud Wilhite is an in-depth look at the story of Hosea and Gomer and was actually one of the books I was reading at the time.) The story in a nutshell is this: Hosea was a prophet whom God told to marry a prostitute, Gomer. He was obedient, and they married and had several children. But over the course of time, Gomer kept going back to her life of prostitution and shame no matter how well Hosea loved her and no matter how hard he pursued her. All of this culminates in Gomer being sold into slavery and Hosea buying her back and eventually restoring her to her position as his wife. (And everyone lives, presumably, happily ever after.)

Can you imagine? First being told by *God* to marry a prostitute and actually being obedient and doing it? Only then to have your wife keep returning to her life of harlotry instead of embracing the life of hope you offered her? Is this beginning to sound familiar to anyone? Perhaps because God offers us a life of restoration in Him and instead, time and time and time again, we willingly choose to return to the ruin of our sin.

Oh, what a beautiful God He is. What a gracious, loving, wildly forgiving, and even flagrantly merciful God He is. And how He pursues us! Through our sin, our shame, our rebellion, our mess—He never stops seeking after us. *He* chases after *us*.

CAN YOU EVEN FATHOM A GOD WHO DOESN'T WAIT FOR HIS CHILDREN TO COME TO HIM BUT UNABASHEDLY PURSUES THEM?

I had become a woman after God's own heart . . . only to discover He was a God after mine.

But why the tug at my heart to read this story *now*? Why did Gomer and Hosea keep popping up everywhere I looked? And why did I feel as if it was somehow all intrinsically linked to Mr. E's return to my life? I decided to turn to the one place where I knew I'd find the answers: God.

This was during the season when I was just learning how to *truly* spend quiet time with God. The early days of my fireside chats with Jesus. They were beautiful days. You know how sometimes you're just in the sweet spot with God and His presence is palpable and

His voice recognizable and His will discernable? The Holy Spirit was on the move in my life, and I knew He had something important to share with me.

So I asked Him one night during quiet time: "God, what does all this mean? Why do you keep bringing me back to the book of Hosea? What is it You want me to see? And why is Mr. E back in my life after all this time? What is his greater purpose in my life?"

And then I sat quietly, in hopeful anticipation, and waited. Waited in the silence, in the stillness, in the uncertainty. Waited for God to speak.

"*I needed you to see, Mandy.*" I felt the familiar tug at my heart. Not a tangible voice, but a stirring in my spirit, and I knew He was speaking straight to my heart.

"See what, Lord?"

"*I needed you to see that the way Mr. E has been with you over the years—up and down and in and out and committed to you and then running from you—is the way you've been with Me.*"

I was left speechless. Thoughtless. Breathless. I guess that's what happens when God speaks.

And suddenly it all came into focus. The way I had been somewhat halfhearted in my relationship with God since I had turned my life over to Him years ago at age twenty. The times I had run from Him. The times I had gotten so on fire for Him I could hardly sit still, only to get distracted a few months later and wander off the path again. The times I had chased after Him and then given up when I didn't feel it was possible to ever truly catch Him or lost my desire to truly catch Him at all. The times I had allowed rebellion and sin and pride and my own weak humanity and flesh to keep me from serving Him. The times I had ignored Him altogether. The same way Mr. E had kept one foot in and one foot out of my life for seven long years. It suddenly all made so much sense. Oh, how I must have broken God's heart.

And then . . .

"*I want you to pursue Me the way you want a man to pursue you.*" Wow.

Of course, instead of taking a moment to allow *that* monumental statement to settle, in all of my ridiculous, stubborn foolishness, I had to pipe up: "But God!"

"But God! *Seven years*? You needed Mr. E to stick around and rake me over the coals for *seven years*? Couldn't You have maybe taught me the lesson in, I don't know . . . three years?"

I *swear* I felt Him laugh.

"*Mandy. Look up the biblical significance of the number seven.*"

I probably huffed and puffed a few times in frustration, but then I obliged . . . because when God tells you to do something, I was learning you should shut up and do it.

To my surprise, I quickly discovered that not only was the number seven significant in the Bible, it's quite arguably the *most* significant number in the Bible, mentioned more than seven hundred times.

And then I saw the definition. And I laughed out loud. And then I wept. And then I laughed again. And then I recorded a voice memo on my phone reading the definition to myself so I would never forget this moment, this revelation, this conversation with God.

Seven is a number of completeness. It is divine perfection or something that is finished, such as the week of creation in Genesis.

Then the stirring in my spirit, one final time.

"The seventh year will be the 'Year of Completion' for you and Mr. E," God whispered to my heart.

And then He was gone. His presence lifted. His Spirit silent. And my heart at peace.

Because all of a sudden I knew. It all made perfect sense.

One way or another, the relationship between Mr. E and me would be decided this year. Had I paid closer attention to the third part of the biblical definition of the number seven, the "something that is finished" part, I would have known right then and there which way it was going to go. But it wasn't time to know. This wasn't the moment for me to know. This was the moment for the beautiful uncertainty of walking with God and trusting that in His perfect timing, I would come to know.

And I would.

BEAUTIFUL CERTAINTY:

I ask God for clarity a lot. Just last night I wrote in my prayer journal: "Please show me, God. Please make it very, very, very clear" about something I've been praying about. And then I woke up to this Scripture passage as the Verse of the Day: "Lean not on your own understanding" (Proverbs 3:5 NIV). As human beings, we want constant understanding and clarity about every single little thing in God's plan, and sometimes we're just not meant to understand Him. Sometimes we're simply called to seek Him and to trust Him and then to let go, because He can handle any situation much better than we ever could.

Prayer

God, I surrender it all to You and trust You'll give back what is meant for me or keep it safe until I'm ready for it.

Advent, Waiting, and Singleness

It can be easy as a single woman to feel a bit alienated from the mainstream Christmas traditions since they are mostly family oriented in nature and often serve to remind us singles we don't yet have a family. We shop for Christmas presents alone, we decorate our trees alone, we stand under numerous bundles of mistletoe alone and pray Creepy McCreeperson from the office party won't choose this moment to make his move. (Because in the holiday movie of our lives, the male lead rarely ever looks like Jude Law.)

But I digress.

The truth is that as much as I love Christmas (And I do love Christmas. You should see my apartment every year. It looks like Santa's Workshop. On steroids.), I always find it a little difficult to find the commonality between the holiday season and the single season.

Until I started really studying the meaning of Advent.

Obviously Advent in the Christian tradition is the four Sundays preceding Christmas. But the actual definition of the word is much more telling:

Advent—an arrival or coming, especially one which is awaited

Advent is waiting in expectation for something that's a long time in coming. And although we are obviously waiting in expectation for the day we celebrate our Savior's birth, maybe Advent can also be a reminder of the importance of waiting for anything we hope for, long for, pray for.

And who can better understand *waiting* than single women?

I've never been a great waiter. I abhor sitting in traffic. I tap my toe impatiently waiting for a movie or a concert to start and eat my way through my entire box of Junior Mints before the previews even come on. And don't even get me started on waiting in line at Chick-fil-A. (Seriously, the line is wrapped around the building day or night, rain or shine. Really, what is in those nuggets that makes them so addictive?)

But most of all, on the cusp of the new year, I found myself weary of waiting for love.

I was weary of having no one to cook for (I never

thought *that* day would come!). I was weary of not having a partner to back me up when the oil change place tried to convince me I needed a new filter, new wiper blades, a new engine, and a partridge in a pear tree. I was weary of not having a "tribe." I was weary of buying wedding and baby shower gifts for other people (sorry, friends—it's true). I was weary of the endless parade of adorable family photos of fun holiday happenings that besiege my social media timelines around the holidays. I was weary of sitting alone and going places alone. I was weary of having no one to share my heart and my life and my love with.

I loved my life. I was content in my singleness. I didn't doubt my completeness or my value as a single person. But I was ready for the next chapter of my life and all the experiences it would bring, and I was weary of waiting for it.

IF ADVENT IS A SEASON THAT CELEBRATES THE ACT OF WAITING, ISN'T IT POSSIBLE THERE IS SOMETHING SACRED IN THE WAITING THAT GOD WANTS TO SHARE WITH US?

Waiting and God's silence seem to go hand in hand. It's not called "Silent Night" for nothing. Isn't there something there that should tell us that while hoping for the miracle, while praying for the miracle, while waiting for the miracle, maybe we should view God's silence not as punishment but as preparation? Maybe we should stop cursing the waiting and start thanking God for it. Maybe we should trust that His timing and His way are perfect and He's only asking us to wait because He loves us too much to bring us something we're not yet ready for. "Long lay the world, in sin and error pining . . .'til He appeared, and the soul felt its worth." —from "O Holy Night"

LONG WE WAIT FOR THE PROMISE. BUT WE DO NOT WAIT ALONE. HE IS THERE, IN THE WAITING, IN THE PRAYING, IN THE WEEPING, IN THE HOPING, IN THE DOUBTING, IN THE TRUSTING, IN THE WISHING. HE IS THERE.

My hope—for me and for you and for all single women and really anyone wishing and hoping and praying for a miracle at Advent season—is to embrace the beautiful uncertainty of waiting. If it seems as if God is silent, maybe it's because it's your turn to talk. Tell Him your doubts, your fears, your dreams. Then wait. Wait with expectation for His arrival. I can't tell you when, how, or even *if* your dream or my dream of love or marriage or babies or being a published writer or whatever your biggest wish is will come true. But I can assure you that no matter what happens, He will be with us in the midst of it.

And it will be beautiful.

BEAUTIFUL CERTAINTY:

I often need to be reminded that God's timetable is better than mine. The in-between, the mean-time, the waiting—it can all be frustrating, but it is in those moments we are refined, redesigned, and realigned with God's will as He prepares us to be launched into our next chapter.

Prayer

God, help me to sit patiently in times of waiting, knowing I am being prepared for what I'm waiting for. Thank You for keeping me from receiving a blessing or entering into a season I'm not yet ready for.

Getting Uncomfortable

*D*uring my quiet time with God at the first of the year, God spoke something very clearly into my heart:

"Get uncomfortable this year, Mandy. You worship comfort too much."

Now I *knew* that had to come from Him, because who wants to hear a statement like that? Who would choose to tell that to themselves? "Get uncomfortable"? My idea of uncomfortable is to walk to the mailbox instead of driving. I quite enjoy being comfortable, thank you very much. My favorite place on earth is my cozy apartment, wearing a onesie, drinking cocoa, and watching Netflix. A proverbial Mandy-made *womb* of comfort. So getting uncomfortable? Not high on my list of fun things to do.

Still, everywhere I looked there seemed to be signs pushing me out of my comfort zone. I went to see the movie *The Secret Life of Walter Mitty*, which if you haven't seen it, you should, immediately. It's all about a normal, unassuming man who grows weary of living his normal, unassuming life and strikes out on a fantastical journey that winds up altering the course of the rest of his life, and the movie only confirmed my feeling that my reckless pursuit of God was going to carry me a little farther away from home this year than I might have anticipated. I was feeling increasingly restless, like God was calling me to something *big*, but I wasn't sure to what.

Until a few days later when I woke up with a word on my lips. "RV." I said it out loud to myself as soon as I opened my eyes one morning in early January. "Wait. RV? As in 'recreational vehicle'?" I wasn't sure if I had dreamed about it or if it was something God had whispered into my spirit, but either way, it seemed odd. And it intrigued me.

What could this mean? RV? My experience with RVs was somewhat limited at the time. Although my family had briefly owned one a few years prior, the extent of our actual camping prowess began and ended in the parking lot of Walmart, where my parents and I decided to "go on an adventure" by spending the night there one night. After my dad wouldn't stop snoring, my mom wouldn't stop peeking out the window looking for serial killers, and I couldn't justify attempting to sleep on a "bed" that consisted of a one-inch-thick padding stretched across a hard table when my *actual* comfy bed was less than three miles away, we packed it up and called it a night.

This time, though, felt different. As I prayed and pondered it in my heart, I started to feel the stirrings of—dare I say it?—a plan coming together. I had followers and readers and fans of *The Single Woman* all over the country (and actually all over the world, but I doubted if I could trot across the ocean in an RV). How great would it be to finally meet some of them face-to-face? My second book was coming out in just two months. And my friend and fellow single woman Jaime Jamgochian, a Christian recording artist with a message very similar to mine, had just mentioned to me recently that she had a strange gap in her traveling schedule throughout early spring that she wasn't sure how to fill. I was starting to sense that God was calling the two of us to go out on the road and minister to single women. But I had no idea where to begin. Plus, I was terrified to mention it to Jaime, for fear she would laugh in my face.

Which she did. Loudly. And for several (long) minutes when I called her to spill my heart and vision to her a night or two later. To her credit, I'm guessing the reason she got such a cackle out of the idea the first time I shared it with her is because my original plan included us, just the two of us, renting an RV and driving it around the country ourselves. Just Jaime and me.

Two crazy blondes on the open road with absolutely no structure or plan or itinerary. I should mention I have absolutely zero business sense or acumen for taking a crazy plan and turning it into an actual organized, working venture. But God placed Jaime and I together because, as a touring musician of more than a decade, she did.

After she laughed long and hard, Jaime agreed to pray about it. (Again, to her credit, she didn't shoot me down completely. She was quite diplomatic.) I agreed to keep praying about it. And the two of us made plans to touch base in a day or two to see where we both stood.

An amazing thing happened in that next couple of days. God completely moved in both my heart and Jaime's heart, and by the time we came back together, we knew. We had a beautiful certainty that only the God of the universe could have placed in both our hearts in the midst of complete and total uncertainty.

We didn't know how it was going to all come together. We didn't know where the RV or the money for food and hotels and gas was going to come from. We didn't even know where we would go because we had zero tour dates lined up. (I had never even really been a formal speaker with actual speaking dates.) We just knew we were to *go*. To move. To start taking steps on faith and to trust God to do the rest.

Less than two months later, we would find

ourselves in that RV I dreamed about, doing the very things both Jaime and I envisioned: Ministering to women. Speaking life and hope to women. Sharing the gospel with women. But on that cold winter day, we never could have imagined all the ways God would supernaturally work on our behalf to create something from nothing.

But He did. And that's how The Sass, Class & Compassion Tour was born. On a wing and a prayer.

As most beautifully uncertain miracles are.

EXERCISE: GET UNCOMFORTABLE FOR GOD

What are some ways you can "get uncomfortable" for God? It doesn't have to be something big or fancy or complicated. Oftentimes, even small steps can make a difference in your life, the lives of those around you, your church, your community, or even the world.

1. *Brainstorm*. Make a list of ideas of ways you can push yourself outside your comfort zone for God.
2. *Pray*. Spend some time meditating and praying over the list to see which idea or ideas seem to speak to your heart the most. Once

you've identified which of your ideas you want to focus on, ask a close friend or trusted prayer partner to pray over it with you, and ask God to show you how to proceed to turn your dream into a reality.

3. *Wait*. If I learned nothing else from my big adventure with Jaime, it was that a big God-dream requires big patience. There would be days during the midst of all the logistical planning when we would be tempted to move forward with a decision and something in our spirit would hold us back or just wouldn't feel right. So we would come together and pray about it and then wait for an answer; and every time, God would come through. Even if whatever we were coming up against at that moment looked impossible. There were dozens of times God could have closed the door on the idea of our tour completely, and although we would have been sad to surrender our dream, we would have done so. Nothing, no matter how well intentioned or inspiring or bold, can be carried out without God's blessing and His perfect timing.

4. *Act*. Start making calls, sending e-mails, doing outreach, writing, singing, planning, dreaming, working, *doing*. Take bold steps on behalf

of your God-dream. Whatever happens, stepping out in faith and trusting God to show up will change you. It will change the lives of the people around you. That's what faith does. It moves you, shakes you, challenges you, stretches you, and shatters your comfort zone . . . and with it, the limitations you place on God. When a God-dream meets faith, miracles happen. And no one who witnesses it is ever the same.

PART TWO

Spring

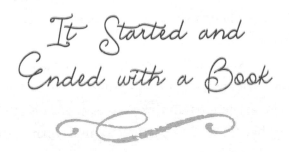

It Started and Ended with a Book

*I*t all started with a little girl and a book.

It was called *Peppermint Fence*. She ran home clutching the book to her chest like gold, proudly showing it off to her parents and big sister. She was the first person in her first-grade class to take home a real book. She was so excited that she read the entire book in one night (only the first of thousands of times she would do this).

Through the years, the little girl grew, and she changed. She shot up several inches. Glasses took over her face and braces her teeth. Nothing about this little girl from one day to the next was a constant. Nothing, that is, except her love of reading. During the beautiful uncertainty of growing up, she went from *Peppermint Fence* to *Harold and the Purple Crayon* to *Pollyanna* to *Anne of Green Gables* to *The Baby-Sitters Club* to *Sweet Valley High*. She traveled to Oz and Narnia and Deep

South Atlanta, where she lost her heart to Captain Rhett Butler. As she grew, her beloved characters grew with her. Although the cast was constantly changing, her love of the written word never wavered.

At times through the years, she would set aside her fictional friends and turn to other books to help her through the bumps and bruises of life. The self-help aisle in her favorite bookstore became worn with the tread of her heels, as she paced back and forth to find the perfect book to match her not-so-perfect moments. She learned how to know if a boy was "just not that into her." She embraced *The Power of Positive Thinking*. She even "kissed dating good bye" for a while based on the concept in a popular book, but after years of no dating (and subsequently, no kissing), she grew frustrated and kissed the book good-bye instead.

When she was twenty, she met the love of her life. His name was Jesus. When her first love, a brave boy serving in the Marine Corps, heard about this (although they were long since broken up), he promptly mailed to her what would become her favorite book, both for literary and sentimental purposes. *Mere Christianity* by C. S. Lewis—the same author who had taught her about believing in magic when she was a little girl through a certain lion, witch, and wardrobe. The more the girl read this book, and other books like it, the more she fell in love with God. It made sense, you know. There was nothing this girl loved more than the written word, and as another of the girl's favorite books taught her, Jesus was and is "the Word made flesh."

She fell away from God over the next several years, but always, always, the "Word made flesh" drew her back to Him with . . . what else? The written word. She read about how *Twelve Ordinary Men* changed the course of history. She learned *What Jesus Meant*. She even followed Him, weeping, to the cross as *He Chose the Nails*. He came alive to her in the pages of those books, reaching off the page to wipe her tears, mend her heart, and comfort her troubled spirit.

After every trial the girl faced in life, she turned to a book. Sometimes it was for comfort. Sometimes it was for wisdom. Sometimes it was purely for escapism (that's what she blames her addiction to the Left Behind and Twilight series on, anyway). Sometimes it was to visit some place she'd never been, like when she ate and prayed and loved with Elizabeth Gilbert all the way through Italy, India, and Indonesia and took a walk on the *Wild* side with Cheryl Strayed on the Pacific Crest Trail. Books were her constant companion, her source of comfort, the very foundation of her creativity.

But then one day, after the girl had endured a particularly painful heartbreak, for the first time in her life, she didn't turn to a book.

She picked up a pen and wrote one instead.

With that pen, with her dozens of beloved characters and protagonists and antagonists and literary legends watching fondly from the corners of her heart, and armed with the power of a thousand stories she had gotten lost in over the years, she found herself. Right there in the midst of the words she had spent her entire life searching for her voice in . . . she finally found it.

It ended with a not-so-little girl and a book.

For you see, she walked by her favorite bookstore one day, and there in the window was a great big display that read "Author Mandy Hale, Talk/Signing, March 11, 2014."

Among the same shelves that house her helpers, her friends, her inspirations, and her heroes, now stands her book. And as she gazes proudly at the tears, heartbreaks, triumphs, wins, losses, and beautiful uncertainty of her story pressed between the pages, she can finally see how every word she read and step she took along the way gave her the courage to stand where she does today.

BEAUTIFUL CERTAINTY:

God allows us to make our own plans. However, if we are truly submitted to the lordship of Jesus, He comes alongside us and orders our steps according to His plan, not ours. I've been walking with Him long enough to know He will let me choose my own way if I want to, and He won't fight me on it. And it might even be a good way. But when I surrender to Him completely and say, "Not my will, but Yours be done," He is able to do way above and beyond anything I could ever do on my own! After all, He is the author of our dreams.

AND WHEN WE ARE WILLING TO HAND HIM THE PEN TO OUR LIVES, HE WRITES A MUCH MORE BEAUTIFUL STORY THAN WE COULD EVER ASK FOR OR IMAGINE.

Prayer

Thank You, God, that You always knew who I was long before I did. Thank You that You know the plans You have for me, plans to prosper me and not to harm me, plans to give me hope and a future—and sometimes to make even my biggest dreams come true (Jeremiah 29:11).

Family and Grace I Never Knew

Suddenly, it was spring, and new beginnings had arrived. My second book, *I've Never Been to Vegas but My Luggage Has,* was released, and we had a big launch party, drawing people from all different chapters of my life. It was a beautiful thing.

The faces I was perhaps most excited to see in the crowd were those of my dad's side of the family: aunts and cousins we had only just learned about the year before. Yes, in a headline ripped straight from an episode of *Oprah*, my dad had recently reconnected with his two sisters whom he'd never known, and the story was truly one of healing, redemption, and God's unimaginable grace.

You see, my dad grew up in poverty. He was a "wrong side of the tracks kid" in every sense of the phrase. As a boy, he even literally lived just over the railroad tracks that divided the "good" side of town from the "bad" side of town. He and his brother grew up without a father. My grandfather was never married to my grandmother, and although he came to visit my dad and his brothers on occasion, my dad never really knew him or knew much about him. And because my grandfather died three years before I was born, I, in turn, never knew him or knew much about him either.

As I got older I learned more of the story. My grandfather had been a well-respected and beloved figure in a small town several miles down the road from the town where my dad grew up and where I have lived essentially my whole life. My grandfather had a wife and a family—five daughters, to be exact—in his small town, and was city court clerk for a time. He had a reputation for being a wonderful man: giving, tenderhearted, generous. He also had flaws and weaknesses, as all of us do. His flaw happened to be that he had a wife and five daughters in one town and a mistress and two sons in another.

My grandfather died in 1975, and the lives of each of his families carried on. Separately. My dad and his brother knew about their five sisters just down the road, but they never dared to reach out to them. The shame of being the "wrong side of the tracks" family stayed with them, even as they grew up and raised their own families on the right side of the tracks. My dad, raised in abject poverty and without a real father figure to teach him how to be a man, put himself (and his two daughters) through college, and then he went on to law school. He is the most beautiful example of a dad that I know: Unconditional. Selfless. Grace filled. Only in looking back now can I see that my dad's choice of a legal career was likely a subconscious need to follow in the footsteps of the father he never knew. A father, I know, who would have been so proud of his boy . . . had he taken the chance to really know him.

About two years ago, a young girl ran up to my dad one day on the town square, and much to his surprise, asked if he were her great-uncle. Yes, as it turned out, my dad's sisters knew about him and his brother after all. And they not only knew *about* the brothers, they wanted to actually *know* them. Only two of the five sisters were still alive, but my dad's great-niece quickly put him in touch with one of the sisters, my wonderful Aunt Myra. A few weeks later, my dad and his brother (with me tagging along) set out to meet an entire family we had never known.

I'll never forget how wonderful it was that day to see these three gray-haired siblings meet and share and cry and embrace. One sister who had been loved, cared for, and accepted. Two brothers who had not. And a long-gone father whom they all loved but could all admit they never really knew. Myra did tell us that my grandfather had given his life to God five years before he passed. He confessed his transgressions to his wife and went to his grave peacefully. That news must have given my dad and my uncle a good deal of comfort.

Myra explained they had known about their brothers all along but, like my dad and my uncle, had been afraid to approach them. They weren't sure how my dad and my uncle would feel about them, the daughters who had been raised with two parents instead of just one. She also gave my dad a great gift that day by telling him: "We never blamed you. We can't control what our parents did. You were children. It wasn't your fault."

I watched the weight of years of questions, shame, and self-doubt lift off my dad's shoulders with those words. At age sixty, he was finally embraced, proverbially and literally, by one of his sisters and, by extension, his father—the man he never knew but desperately wanted to. All people need to be validated by their dads. My dad lived much of his life without that validation. To see grace fall and to see his shoulders, head, and self-worth rise was nothing short of a miracle.

And I got a gift too. As I learned about my aunts, both the ones still here and the ones who had passed, I began to recognize myself in them. My aunt Jewell, who passed away a few years back, sounded especially feisty. Myra told us the story of how Jewell once tossed her boyfriend out of the car on the way back from Florida because he was treating her disrespectfully. He had to find his way to a bus station, and it took him a full three days to make his way home. But he never treated Jewell poorly again after that!

As Myra relayed story after story of these strong, spirited aunts of mine, it was as though the final piece of the puzzle of *me* clicked into place. I had never really been able to determine where my sass came from, as the women on my mom's side of the family tend to be more traditional and conservative. But finally, here was my answer. Turns out I came from a long line of colorful, feisty, independent women. The beautiful uncertainty of my heritage was now beautifully certain. And I couldn't have been prouder.

These people, these aunts and cousins and uncles I never knew, were also fiercely loyal. When my second book released in March 2014, they came out in droves to my book launch. It touched my heart and moved me beyond words to see how they had each other's backs and now my family's backs as well. We were welcomed, supported, and celebrated without question. And through them, I saw through the veil to get a peek at God's grace. His furious love for us. His lack of conditions. His determination to reconcile with us, no matter what it takes.

From the seeds of hurt and shame and rejection and sin . . . rose a new family.

Yes, it was spring, and new beginnings had arrived.

BEAUTIFUL CERTAINTY:

We can't control where we came from or who our parents are. We can't control how we were raised. But we *can* control where we go from here. And we can ask God for the strength to see our parents and our families through His eyes. We *can* forgive. We can let people off the hook because every time we do, it's really us who swims a little faster.

My dad had every right to use his childhood and the lack of a dad and the poor conditions he lived in as an excuse to rebel and rage against the machine, and maybe even go on to neglect his own children. And my aunts could have easily chosen the path of blaming my dad and his brother for the two men's very existence. But instead, both sides chose *grace*. Both sides chose to accept that their father was flawed, but that didn't make him irredeemable. They chose to walk in forgiveness and love, and because of that, two families that could have viewed themselves as forever damaged and scarred and given a raw deal came together and formed one family of togetherness and solidarity and peace.

I don't know your past, and I am certain some of you have been through some unimaginable things at the hands of family members you loved. I'm not saying what they did was right. I am saying this:

YOU ARE STRONGER AND BIGGER AND BRAVER THAN WHAT THEY DID, AND YOU DON'T HAVE TO LET IT DEFINE YOU ANY LONGER. FORGIVE. LET GO. MOVE ON. DON'T LOOK BACK. YOUR NEW BEGINNING IS WAITING.

Prayer

God, I lift up my past and everything that happened to me to You, and I ask You to redeem it. I choose to forgive _____, let them off the hook, and move on with my life. I choose to walk in grace. I choose peace of mind over clinging to the past. I refuse to let anyone's wrongdoing keep me stuck. Thank You for the strength to stop reliving my past, to start living my present, and to walk in the certainty of knowing my future lies with You.

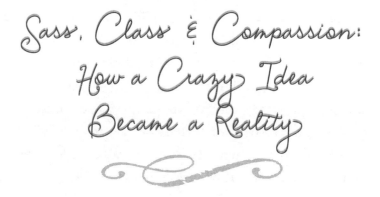

Sass, Class & Compassion: How a Crazy Idea Became a Reality

When we left off in my "God Adventure," Jaime and I were praying about our crazy idea to hit the open road in an RV to speak to women at live events across the country. Just three problems: we didn't own an RV, we had exactly zero live events on the books, and we had no budget or clue as to how we would pay for this nationwide jaunt.

But God had told me to get uncomfortable in 2014. And nothing at that point in my life made me more uncomfortable than asking people for big, bold favors. Asking God for big, bold favors was one thing. Asking other people, feeling like an imposition to them, feeling like I was forcing myself on them, was an entirely different matter.

And yet I knew in my heart this was an adventure

God was calling me on. A faith journey. He was beckoning me out of the boat and daring me to walk on water. Would I keep my eyes on Him and continue walking forward in trust? Or would I look around at our circumstances and the daunting task of the bold *ask* and sink from doubt and timidity? Jaime and I both knew our mission was clear: to travel the country and speak to women, pray with women, share our testimonies with women, encourage women. So how could we let fear stand in the way of allowing God to provide?

We knew transportation had to come first, and because I had the term *RV* emblazoned on my heart, we both felt this was the mode of transportation God wanted to provide for us. After much thought and prayer, Jaime reached out to a precious lady, Pam, whom she knew owned an RV, loved God, and had an adventurous spirit. Pam was a fan of Jaime's music, and although they had only met twice before in their lives, Jaime knew Pam would take our request seriously and consult the Holy Spirit on the matter (rather than just guffaw at us, as a lot of our friends and family were doing). I'll admit, it probably sounded like a harebrained scheme in those early days of planning, and yet Pam didn't laugh at us. She listened to us and to our hearts, and she agreed to give our idea serious consideration and prayer over the next few days.

In the meantime, Jaime and I went to work on booking tour dates, turning to our social-media platforms to gauge the interest in bringing our tour to churches, schools, and cities across the country.

Well, I can definitely say if I had never before believed the Scripture verse that says He "is able to do exceedingly abundantly above all that we ask or think" (Ephesians 3:20 NKJV), I became a believer during those days.

Within a few days, Pam came back and said not only did she want to give us the use of her brand-new, luxury RV, but she also wanted to come with us as our unofficial "tour mama." Plus, she would cover the costs of all of our fuel. *Plus* hire a driver for us. (Which was a massive relief. I'm not exactly known for my sense of direction.)

The wonderful organization Compassion International heard about what we were doing and almost immediately agreed to come on board as our official tour partners.

A dear friend of mine, Ben, whom I had met on Twitter a few years prior and had become the best of friends with during hours of text and phone conversations, joined the motley crew as our road manager. We'd never met in person until the tour, which shows you the power of social media. (And also the power of prayer. Thank you, Lord, that Ben turned out to be wonderful and completely normal and not a serial killer.)

A generous reader of mine sent us a check in the mail to cover our food budget and any incidentals we might have along the way.

And then, one day in late January, we booked our first official tour date. At Lakewood Church. As in Joel Osteen's church. As in the *biggest* church in the country. And then we booked seven more events across the US, along with media events, meet-ups, and a book signing in Washington, DC.

Then two days after the book launch for *I've Never Been to Vegas but My Luggage Has* in mid-March, there was nothing left to do but *go*. So we did. Me, Jaime, Pam, Ben, and Harold (our driver). Our colorful little family for the next three and a half weeks. What had started as a crazy idea was now a reality.

Although I was by no means a God expert, but just a novice who longed to draw near Him and know His heart more and more, the conception and planning of The Sass, Class & Compassion Tour taught me that GOD. DOESN'T. PLAY.

WHEN HE WANTS YOU TO DO SOMETHING, HE DRIVES YOU CRAZY UNTIL YOU DO IT. AND THEN WHEN YOU RISE UP AND MEET HIS PLANS WITH YOUR OBEDIENCE . . . MIRACLES HAPPEN.

I had never been away from the Nashville, Tennessee, area for longer than eight days at a time. I had never tried to live on an RV. My knees shook, and my heart raced at the thought of standing up in front of hundreds and even thousands of women night after night and hopefully getting out of the way and letting God speak through me. (Public speaking, while I had done it many times, never seemed to become any easier for me.) But the whole "living on the edge" with God thing . . . wow. It was worth every last bit of the risk. It was worth the fear. It was worth acknowledging that I was a weak, imperfect vessel, admitting my shortcomings, and allowing Him to use me anyway . . . because as His Word tells us, His strength is made perfect in our weakness (2 Corinthians 12:9). And so I resolved to myself, and to Him, to do it afraid. To chase after His presence and His will and His ways and to trust that everything else would work itself out.

And bumping along the highway in that RV to our first tour date in Maryland, I didn't know if I would ever be able to go back to a normal, ho-hum, polite Christian existence. Because once you've pursued Him through throngs of people to grab hold of the hem of His cloak and He has turned to face you and acknowledged your faith by performing great miracles in your life, the idea of fading back into the crowd and going back to business as usual just no longer appeals. I wanted even more of Him. I wanted more of this wild adventure of leaping and trusting Him to catch me. I wanted more risk and fear and potential failure. It might sound crazy, but it was true.

IT'S ONLY WHEN YOU'RE WILLING TO WALK ON THE EDGE
WITH HIM THAT HE CAN *TRULY* SHOW YOU THE VIEW.

EXERCISE: THE BOLD ASK

Swallow your pride and your fear and your self-doubt and make a bold ask. Maybe it's for your dream job. Maybe it's for a date. Maybe it's for a raise or for a healing or for someone's forgiveness. Ask *someone* something bold and daring and unexpected. Even if it's asking something from God. Actually, especially then. Step out into the unknown, find something that absolutely terrifies you to ask for and resolve to do it afraid if you have to, but *ask*. The worst answer you can get is no, and your life will go on. The best answer is *yes*—and your life could change forever.

Beautiful Uncertainty

It's Hard to Be a Pigeon in a Seagull World

We were wandering along the beach during the Virginia Beach stop of the tour one day when I got to observe some interesting behavior in the bird world. I love sitting on the beach throwing crumbs to the seagulls (you can imagine that the beach patrons who find themselves beside me are thrilled with this habit), and as we watched a flock of seagulls eagerly peck up the breadcrumbs, suddenly two pigeons appeared.

Pigeons, as you probably know, get a bad rap overall in the animal kingdom. They are often viewed as dumb, unattractive, annoying creatures, not really serving a purpose or adding any color or beauty to the world. And it was clear to see that in the pecking order of life, these two pigeons ranked far below the seagulls. Every time we would try to throw a crumb to the pigeons, they would miss it, be too slow to get it, or get sharply chirped at (scolded) by the overzealous seagulls. Not a single crumb we tossed made it into the beak of one of the pigeons. They were essentially failing at life, and it was discouraging to watch.

Yet . . .

Long after the seagulls gave up and departed our section of the beach for sandier (and crumbier) pastures, the pigeons remained. They hung in there for the good fight and stubbornly refused to give up on the hope that eventually a crumb would find its way to their beaks. And when I discovered a virtual gold-mine of crumbs in a wadded up Starbucks wrapper in my beach bag, guess who was still there to get it? Yep. The pigeons. Those stubborn, hopeful, faith-filled, late-blooming pigeons. I even snapped a picture of the pigeons feasting on their unexpected Starbucks spread as one lone seagull stood by looking confused. The pigeons ended up getting far more crumbs that day than any of the seagulls. Why? Because of their determination not to let their pigeon status hold them back from stepping into the blessings meant for them. And their willingness to wait, patiently, when it looked like nothing was going their way.

Okay, so that might be a tad dramatic since we're discussing pigeons here, but how many of us have had our share of "pigeon moments"? I know I have! I'd venture to say that none of us can say she's never felt like a pigeon at some point in her life. Ignored. Forgotten. A day late and a dollar short. Too plain. Too colorless. Not as attractive as the next person. Passed over. Left out in the cold. Isn't this how society trains us single ladies to feel about ourselves? Like something is wrong with us and inferior about us that keeps us from stepping into the love that seems to come so easily for others?

I would like to encourage you, my beautiful fellow pigeons, to hang in there. Stand firm. Set your face like flint, and decide right now that you are no longer going to be bullied or defined by the seagulls of life.

YOU ARE NO LONGER GOING TO AGREE WITH WHAT THE WORLD HAS TO SAY ABOUT YOU. YOU ARE GOING TO GET WITH WHAT YOU KNOW ABOUT YOU—THE BEAUTIFUL, STRONG, FAITHFUL WOMAN GOD CREATED YOU TO BE.

Your feast is coming. You won't have to fight for it. You won't have to beg for it. You just have to show up, stand confident in who you are, and claim it! The blessing might not come as fast as you would have wanted or in the way you might have pictured, but it's coming! And it's even bigger and better than you ever imagined.

I say it's time for us pigeons to celebrate our unique "pigeon-ness." Because the thing is, when you get really close to a pigeon, you start to see that what the world thinks about them and says about them has very little to do with who they really are. They have beautiful, brilliantly colored feathers woven in with their under-stated gray ones. Delicate features. And spirits that refuse to be defeated.

I don't know about you, but that makes me rather proud to be a pigeon.

BEAUTIFUL CERTAINTY:

God doesn't wait for us to be perfect to love us, and He doesn't wait for us to be perfect to use us. Actually, He doesn't wait for us to be perfect at all. Whether we're pigeons or seagulls, He meets us right where we're at—in the mess, in the trenches, in the brokenness—and turns us into something beautiful. He sees our potential even when others don't!

Prayer

God, help me to embrace who I am and love who I am, flaws and all, just the way You love me. In those moments when I feel like a pigeon instead of a seagull, help me to see myself through Your eyes. And even in the middle of my most forgotten, uncertain moments, remind me of Your promise that You will cover me with Your feathers, and under Your wings I will find refuge (Psalm 91:4).

Snapshots from the Road

Excerpt from my journal:

It's still dark outside. Everyone in the bus is asleep
except for me and Harold, our driver. Just sitting here
watching the small towns go by and the new day start
to break . . . thinking how fortunate I am to have such
an experience as this. It is one I will treasure forever.

The tour.

So many memories flash through my mind when
I think about the tour. The snowstorm that stranded
us atop a mountain somewhere outside of Shanksville,
Pennsylvania. The day the heater broke in the RV and
left us shaking and shivering our way to New York
City. The 6:00 a.m. bus call that found me sitting in
the passenger's seat next to our driver, Harold, as we
chased the sunrise through the hills of West Virginia.
The beautiful uncertainty of the new day dawning as I
sat, wrapped in a blanket, dreaming and praying and

watching the day break while the rest of the crew slept peacefully behind us.

I remember our event in Bristol, Tennessee, where I sponsored my beautiful, little African girl, Marsani, through Compassion International. And the brilliantly sunny day we strolled through our nation's capital, and the book signing I held at a Barnes and Noble there that turned into a mini-revival, complete with prayer and tears and laughter and everything in between. The event in Pittsburgh where we were expecting seventy-five ladies and instead only seven showed up. The night I sat soaking my tired bones in a bathtub in Manassas, Virginia, eating a red velvet cupcake a dear friend from high school had brought to one of our events and wondering when I had ever been happier. The comradery of our colorful little five-person family, and all the giggles and tears and excitement and fears we shared. The disappointment after an event didn't go so well, and the gleeful celebration when we really knocked one out of the park. The pedicures the five of us got (yes, even the guys!) at a stop in Winslow, Arizona. The faces of all the beautiful ladies who came out to hear Jaime and me share our hearts. The faces of the beautiful ladies who, in turn, shared their hearts with us. I remember every single one.

One of my more precious memories from this

crazy three-and-a-half-week journey was finding a lifelong friend in Ben, my "Twitter friend" turned real-life friend turned road manager. Ben became my little brother, my right-hand man, and, in many ways, my sanity on the tour. We had a routine where every night after the live events, we would sit for hours, eating junk food and recapping the entire evening and cracking ourselves up at things no one else in the world would find funny. Both of us knew how fleeting this magical journey was, and we wanted to relish every moment of it, even if that meant sometimes sacrificing sleep.

That's how Ben and I found ourselves, at 1:00 a.m. on Saint Patrick's Day, wandering through Times Square, sipping hot chocolate, and gazing around in amazement at the City That Never Sleeps. Ben had never been to New York City, and although I had to be up at 5:00 a.m. to prep for an interview with Fox News, I knew that when I looked back on the trip, I wouldn't recall the sleep I missed or how exhausted I was the next day (and I was exhausted). No, what I would remember forever was watching my dear friend's eyes light up at his first glimpse of the crossroads of the world. And today, more than a year later, my heart floods with gratitude that I slept less and lived more on that trip.

BECAUSE THAT'S WHAT LIFE IS ABOUT: CAPTURING THE MOMENT. GRABBING HOLD OF IT AND REFUSING TO LET IT SLIP FROM YOUR GRASP SIMPLY BECAUSE YOU'RE TIRED OR INCONVENIENCED OR IN A HURRY.

Making sweet memories you can take out of the scrapbook of your heart on rainy days for years to come, finding laughter, love, comfort, and joy among its pages.

I remember my note cards from the trip. My safety net. My security system to warn panic and anxiety to *steer clear* when I was standing onstage in front of hundreds and even thousands of women. Index cards that detailed what I was supposed to say during my talk. At the beginning of the tour, I didn't see how I could make it through even five minutes of one event without them. What if I went blank? What if I forgot what to say? What if I had a massive panic attack onstage in front of everyone?

Every night before we took the stage, I said the same simple prayer: "More of You, God. Less of me." And every night, He showed up. He held my hand. He gave me the words to say. He stayed by my side every step of the way. And I didn't have one panic attack. So somewhere between the East-Coast leg and the West-Coast leg of the tour, when God told me to throw the note cards away, step out in faith, and trust Him, I obliged. And by our last and biggest event at Lakewood Church in Houston, I spoke in front of more than one thousand women with clarity and confidence and boldness with nary a note card in sight. Now, I know God didn't show up just because He wanted to make me a confident speaker or keep me from passing out on stage and falling on some poor soul in the front row. It actually wasn't about me at all. I believe He showed up (as He always does) because He had a blessing hidden in the beautiful uncertainty of my messed-up past and many wrong turns and detours for all of those beautiful ladies with the shining eyes and open hearts who showed up each night of the tour. Just as He wants to take the thing that scares you the most and use it to bless others and glorify Him. There is nothing He can't do through you if you show up and are willing. (You can even show up afraid. But *show up*.)

But before Lakewood and the grand finale, there was a little unfinished business to tend to. My luggage had already been to Vegas. Now it was time for me to go too.

BEAUTIFUL CERTAINTY:

The tour taught me that I don't want to merely exist ever again. I want to *live*. I want you to live too.

SO DO THE THING. TAKE THE LEAP. TRY SOMETHING RIDICULOUS, OR CRAZY, OR BRAVE. NO MATTER HOW IT TURNS OUT, YOU WILL NEVER REGRET CHOOSING TO LIVE—WILD, BOLD, AND FREE.

And if you're stepping out in faith in order to do something that will glorify God, despite your own fears and self-doubts and insecurities, He might just show up and show out in a bigger way than you could have ever imagined.

Prayer

God, thank You for not calling me to live life to its fullest. Thank You for challenging me to step out on faith and for giving me the courage to do so. Even when courage looks like simply showing up to the challenge with knees knocking. Thank You that "doing it afraid" is often where the best memories are made.

Trust Without Borders

The first leg of the tour had officially ended. We were en route to California, and I couldn't even wrap my mind around all the places we had been and things we had seen and people we had met in just a short week and a half. It was less than two weeks since we had departed on this adventure, and it felt like a million years ago in some ways. Then again, it also felt like in the blink of an eye it would all be over and the precious moments the five of us, my little road family, had shared would be but a memory. I remember looking out the window and wishing I could hit the pause button and just rest there in that moment, in that RV rocking back and forth on a bumpy road in New Mexico, surrounded by people who had been mostly strangers two weeks ago but who now felt like my band of brothers and sisters.

Somewhere on that road between Washington, DC, New York City, Baltimore, Pittsburgh, Virginia Beach, and all the tiny towns connecting all the places we had been, I had found myself . . . or at least a new version of myself. I had set out to push myself outside my comfort zone, and push I did. In big ways and small ways. Night after night—six nights to be exact—I had stood on that big stage and shared my heart and my testimony, and God had gotten me through it. Now as we headed west to our two biggest events, in Los Angeles and Houston, somewhere in the depths of my soul I heard His gentle whisper: "Well done, my good and faithful servant."

We had taken our journey to hopefully change some lives and inspire a few people along the way, and yet it sometimes felt like I would be the one to walk away from the experience the most changed. I was slowly learning to surrender my control issues (and little did I know then, but God was about to teach me the biggest lesson about control of my life!). I'd had to learn to be more flexible. To have more grace. To get dressed for live events in some of the most random places. (For example, an athletic equipment room at a high school. Not the locker room, mind you, where the athletes prepare for games, but rather the storage space where the various equipment for the athletes is kept. The head football coach was probably even less enthusiastic about it than we were.)

I'd certainly learned to roll with the punches a little more and to trust God to show up when nerves got the best of me and my anxiety threatened to take over. To let go of how I thought something was supposed to happen and instead just let it be what it was . . . or wasn't. To allow myself to be what *I* was or wasn't. And somehow in the middle of the long hours and motion sickness and complete lack of personal space and never enough sleep, I was the happiest I'd ever been in my life.

YOU SACRIFICE SOMETHING FOR HAPPINESS. YOU SACRIFICE COMFORT AND CERTAINTY AND THE WIDE, EASY ROAD AND INSTEAD LIVE IN THE BEAUTIFUL WILDNESS OF CHASING GOD RIGHT TO THE EDGE OF EVERYTHING THAT SEEMS LOGICAL AND SENSIBLE.

And along the way you have adventures you never thought possible and dance to the beat of your own drummer and meet people you'll never forget. You allow your foundations to be shaken up and rearranged until you know you can never, ever go back to the life of safety that once seemed so appealing. That life no longer fits the expanded borders of who you've become.

My go-to song during the entire tour was "Oceans" by Hillsong United because it challenged me to be brave. To step out on faith and wait patiently for God to meet me there. To trust Him completely and without borders.

As we pressed onward toward California, the flat terrain stretched as far as the eye could see. For the first time in my life, I felt as though my trust really was without borders. My faith was without borders. My dreams were without borders.

My life was without borders.

I never knew what was coming up around the next bend, and that was okay. Because sometimes it's good just to rest in the beautiful uncertainty of walking on the edge with God and trusting Him to lead the way.

BEAUTIFUL CERTAINTY:

When God gives you a vision, when He lays something on your heart, see it through. Sometimes following Him looks really, really crazy to everyone else, but when you step out in faith, He will never fail to meet you there.

Prayer

God, help me to let go of my need to know what's going to happen next and to just *trust*. To trust You, to trust Your timing, to trust Your good and perfect plan for my life. Give me trust without borders. When I get scared and start to doubt, help me to remember to trust in You and not to depend on my own understanding. Help me to seek Your will in all I do, and You will show me which path to take (Proverbs 3:5–6).

Shake, Rattle, Roll, and Surrender Control

My Facebook status from March 28, 2014:

> God is so good. Who but He could take a shaking, quaking, scared-to-death, imperfect vessel like me and put me on a stage to shine His light in front of hundreds of ladies night after night?!? So thankful that His strength is made perfect in our weakness!

I like to think God has such a sense of humor.

I have always been a massive control freak. When I'm describing myself to someone, I usually phrase it as "I'm a *bit* of a control freak." But in the spirit of transparency, I will admit here and now that I am a complete and total control freak. I don't like to delegate (which is a real problem, since I run my own business). I don't like to fly because I'm not the one at the controls. Heck,

I don't even like to surrender driving privileges to anyone else, and when I do, I'm a totally annoying backseat driver.

But I had made it my goal to pursue Jesus with radical abandon that year, and part of that pursuit included me stepping out of the way and surrendering the wheel of my life to Him. And oh how He used my first tour to remind me who was actually in the driver's seat!

First, He reminded me that I *literally* wasn't in the driver's seat. For the first few days of the tour, I sat hunched up in a tense, anxious ball of nerves, worried about Harold (our driver's) driving. If he so much as swerved one centimeter, I started clutching my proverbial pearls. I even recruited Jaime and Ben as my co-conspirators in control-freakdom by pointing out to them all the ways Harold was putting our lives in danger. (By the way, he wasn't. I was just unaccustomed to not being the captain of the ship, and my inner control freak was climbing the walls.) Poor Harold. When he got home, he probably had to wash the gray right out of his hair from the stress of dealing with me white-knuckling my way around the RV.

Once I let poor Harold off the hook, I took a good look around me and realized that life on the road was not as amenable to my requests to "slow down!" as Harold was. There were no predictabilities. No constants. No certainties. Things changed not just from day to day, but from moment to moment. Turns out RVs aren't allowed in tunnels in Manhattan, so that made for interesting navigation of the Big Apple! We got lost. Traffic jams delayed us. We'd show up to a venue a half hour before an event started and have to get ready in the bathroom. I curled my hair and put on makeup with no mirror more than once, silently praying I wouldn't take the stage looking like Bozo the Clown. Nothing— and I mean *nothing*—went according to plan. (But then again, does anything in life ever really go according to our plans?)

Still, by the time we made it to California for our next-to-last live event at a church just outside LA (in Brea, to be exact), I was feeling pretty good about myself and my inner control freak. I had become so accustomed to winging it and going with the flow and (dare I say it?) surrendering control that I felt like this tour had finally broken me of my need to control. I was probably even walking the hallways of the church, patting myself and my new-and-improved, easygoing attitude on the back. I even might have been feeling a little smug about it, giving myself credit where credit was certainly not due.

Before we went onstage that night, Jaime and I prayed that God would move mightily in women's hearts during the course of the evening.

And move He did. In the form of a magnitude 5.1

earthquake, which sent all my undue satisfaction in myself right out the window and my inner control freak screaming through the hallways.

We were just about to close the evening's event with a prayer when the room started shaking violently. Never having been in an earthquake, I didn't realize what was happening at first. It was only when women started screaming and diving under the church pews that it hit me. The next thing I knew, Jaime was grabbing my hand and pulling me offstage. One glance above us at the sound equipment swinging back and forth let me know why. The shaking went on for a seemingly endless amount of time (we later found out it was about thirty seconds), and the whole time I remember thinking (1) *This is it. This is how it's going to end*, and (2) *Am I in a Will Smith movie?*

Then abruptly, the earthquake stopped, and the room was eerily quiet. The wonderful pastor's wife, Sherry, made her way to the front of the room to lead us all in prayer and instill a sense of calm in the ladies who remained (many had grabbed their things and darted for the door in the middle of the chaos). Jaime and I, shaking as wildly as the ground had been a moment before, stood there shell-shocked. Then Sherry finished her prayer and turned to us. "And now I'd like to invite Jaime and Mandy to come back up to close us out!"

Oh snap. I was frozen in my tracks. My knees were jelly. I was a quivering bundle of nerves. I was certain if I opened my mouth, nothing but gibberish would come out. Not one single sensible thought was in my head.

But God hadn't failed me yet on this beautifully uncertain journey I was on with Him, so as I always did when I didn't know what else to do, I put one foot in front of the other and started walking.

And I remembered a Scripture passage: "Don't worry about what you'll say or how you'll say it. The right words will be there; the Spirit of your Father will supply the words" (Matthew 10:19–20 THE MESSAGE).

And He did. Although I don't remember now what I said once I made it back up onstage that night, I do know He got me through it, just as He always does.

We found out later that night that the epicenter of the earthquake was in Brea, about a half mile from the church where our event was, and it was the strongest earthquake LA had seen in about twenty years. We were in LA for just about twenty-four hours, and the most powerful earthquake to hit that area in twenty years happened to strike less than a mile from where we stood. I don't know about you, but I don't think that's a coincidence.

The earthquake, the snowstorm in Shanksville, Pennsylvania, the tour, and the entire year was a lesson in learning how to surrender. How to trust. How to stop trying to control and plan and fix and handle and manipulate and just *let go*. How to relax into the sweet, sweet uncertainty of not always knowing where I was going but never doubting for a second He would be with me every step of the way. God was gently and lovingly taking my hands off the wheel of the RV, of my circumstances, of *life* . . . and showing me what pursuing Him with my whole heart really looked like.

When you seek Him first above all else, you might get lost sometimes. You might get detoured. You might get shaken around and roughed up and tested and tried in the fire. You will sometimes be afraid. You will often feel like you don't know what the heck you're doing. You will never be in control because control, as I have learned, is the opposite of faith.

WHEN YOU PURSUE GOD WHOLEHEARTEDLY, YOU WILL ALWAYS FIND HIM. HE CAN ALWAYS BE FOUND BY A SEEKING, SURRENDERED HEART.

After the wind [there was] an earthquake, but the LORD was not in the earthquake; and after the earthquake a fire, but the LORD was not in the fire; and after the fire a still small voice. (1 Kings 19:11–12 NKJV)

BEAUTIFUL CERTAINTY:

It has taken more than a year of time and distance and reflection for me to see this about the Sass, Class & Compassion Tour: Those three and a half weeks that brought that little band of God-loving people together to crisscross the country were *sacred*. All of us sacrificed, leapt, and took time out of our lives and away from our families to step out in faith and trust God to meet us there. And He did. Not just in the lives of the ladies we ministered to but also in our own lives.

I struggled with *major* control issues before the tour. And although I'd love to say I'm completely cured from my need to control post tour, I'm not. But what I learned while living life on the edge of constant surrender for almost a month in an RV is this: Even when things spiral so far out of control that you can't even *see* control from where you're standing, God is there. He's there, in the middle of missed deadlines and detours and anxiety and even natural disasters.

> YOU DON'T HAVE TO FIGURE IT OUT OR MAKE IT WORK OR EVEN BE BRAVE, BECAUSE HE CAN AND HE DOES AND HE WILL. HE IS.

The One who was and is and is to come has got it covered. He is your control in the midst of chaos. No matter what happens, reach for His hand. He's got you. He will never falter, and He will never let you down.

Prayer

Thank You, God, that I don't have to control or fix or plan or stress or fear or doubt or even wonder how it's all going to work out, because You are wonderfully, perfectly in control. Help me to remember You are in the driver's seat on this beautiful journey we are on. Even when I have no idea where we're going or how we're going to get there, You always do.

PART THREE

Summer

The Five Guys Most Girls Will Love at Some Point in Their Lives

1. **The First Love**. Also commonly known as "the High School Sweetheart." This boy is the Kevin to your Winnie. The Cory to your Topanga. The Dawson to your Joey. Sweet, innocent, idealistic—this is the stuff coming-of-age movies are made of. The First Love is probably the first boy you'll ever kiss. (Or at least the first one you'll kiss and feel the earth move.) He might play a sport and wear a letterman jacket. He'll give you his class ring (which is too big, so you'll proudly wrap yarn around it and wear it as badge of honor).

   Some people go on to marry their First Love, and the list ends here for them. Most, however, wave good-bye to him one bittersweet day as life and circumstance pull you in two different directions and growing up comes much too soon. He'll teach you to drive, to kiss, to *love*, to open your heart and trust and take chances, paving the way for all the other loves still to come . . . and then he'll move on.

2. **The One Who Could Have Been** (but the timing was always off). Maybe you met him while one of you was already in a relationship. Maybe every time you started to get close, life or work or something else completely unexpected came between you. Maybe it was simply God watching out for you because He knew the two of you burned too brightly together to ever sustain a lasting spark. The One Who Could Have Been is also often known as "the Big Love." The love that seemed so meant to be, but it wasn't. The one you were sure you'd never recover from, until you did. The One Who Could Have Been . . . but it just wasn't meant to be.

3. **The Bad Boy**. This one will probably steal your heart in your early twenties, in those years when you're trying to figure out who you are and who you want to be, and discovering that your wings seem to come with a side of rebellion. You'll think you can change him, but you can't. (And secretly you won't want to, because if you did, he'd no longer be the boy who stole your heart.) He'll make you

cry as much as or more than he makes you laugh. Underneath it all, you suspect he has a heart of gold (and he probably does), but it will take years and many women after you to uncover it.

HERE'S THE THING ABOUT BAD BOYS: IN THE END, THEY ALWAYS WALK AWAY. BUT THEY DON'T LEAVE YOU EMPTY-HANDED. IN THEIR WAKE WILL BE GIRLS WHO NOW KNOW WHAT THEY WANT OUT OF LOVE AND WHAT THEY WON'T STAND FOR EVER AGAIN.

And they've finally learned how to say, "Thanks, but no thanks" to anyone who doesn't meet that standard.

4. **The One Who Got Away.** This boy will seem perfect, and secretly, you suspect he is. He'll say all the right things, do all the right things, be the very picture of everything you ever imagined you wanted. Except now that you have it, you question if you're ready for that kind of perfection. And chances are, you're not. God knows when you're ready.

So even though the One Who Got Away offers you everything you thought you wanted, he offers nothing you *know* you need. And what you need is more time. Time to date other guys you'll like but won't love. Time to not date at all and just figure out who *you* are. Time to become the woman you're meant to be—the woman you're closer than ever to coming face-to-face with, thanks to the lessons brought to you by four "almost-loves." You're almost ready for him . . . but not quite. So you'll open your hand and set him free, feeling the beautiful double-edged sword of releasing what's good and holding out for what's good for *you*, while secretly wondering for the next few years if, in letting go of the One Who Got Away, you really let go of the One. Except you didn't.

5. **The One**. I haven't met this one yet. I like to think he's a mix of the four loves that came before him. I like to think he's sweet and steadfast like the First Love, and passionate and challenging like the One Who Could Have Been, and a little wild and rough around the edges like the Bad Boy, with the heart for commitment and building a life together like the One Who Got Away. I like to think he's all of them and none of them, all at the same time. I like to think he will person-ify this list and also erase it, using the scattered pieces of my heart he gently reclaims from each of them as the eraser. I like to think he will make me forget about anyone I ever loved or thought I

loved before he came into my life. But I suspect he won't. I suspect he will outshine them without setting fire to their memory altogether. I suspect he will help me see the need for the other loves while also revealing to me in walking, talking form why it never worked out with any of them. He was always my destination. But they were my preparation. And I am silently thankful for every step it took to get me here.

BEAUTIFUL CERTAINTY:

I have a tattoo on my foot that says "Love Is." Ironic since I haven't quite figured it out yet— what romantic love is, that is. I think, though, that what love *isn't* is staying paralyzed on the first step because you're too terrified of where all the other steps might take you.

LOVE ALWAYS, ALWAYS TAKES THE STEP. IT CLIMBS, IT TRAVELS, IT PERSEVERES TO FIND ITS WAY TO YOU. AND THEN IT TAKES YOUR HAND AND JOINS YOU ON YOUR JOURNEY.

Without motives, without conditions, without fail. I think the Bible defines what "Love Is" best in one of my favorite Scripture passages:

> Love is patient and kind. Love is not jealous or boastful or proud or rude. It does not demand its own way. It is not irritable, and it keeps no record of being wronged. It does not rejoice about injustice but rejoices whenever the truth wins out. Love never gives up, never loses faith, is always hopeful, and endures through every circumstance. (1 Corinthians 13:4–7 NLT)

Love is a journey you could take alone if you had to, but I like to think it's all the more sweet climbing life's staircases with four feet. I'd like to think someday I'll meet the One, but just for today, for me (and perhaps even for you), love is:

A BEAUTIFUL SUMMER NIGHT, A COOL BREEZE, A MILLION STARS IN THE SKY, BARE FEET, AND A GOOD BOOK.

Prayer

God, I surrender my heart to You and ask You to keep it safe until it's time for me to give it away. I am grateful for every time I didn't settle for less than Your best for me. In the lonely times and the uncertain times, help me to remember that with You, nothing—especially love—arrives too soon or too late, but right on time.

Vegas, Tennessee, and Me

I'm weary of talking about Mr. E. I've given him far too many sentences in my story already. But since God told me before 2014 even started that this would be the "Year of Completion" for Mr. E and me, I suppose I need to tell you how that prophetic word came true.

And, oh, how it did come true.

Very long story short . . . Mr. E was in Vegas on a work assignment when I arrived there on our tour stop. Yes, by some weird, random twist of fate (although it wasn't really weird or random at all because looking back I can see how God's hand was all over it), he arrived in Vegas a few weeks after I started planning the tour. So, just to bring you up to speed, that means the romantic lead of my book *I've Never Been to Vegas but My Luggage Has* was *living* in Vegas at the time the book came out. The truth really is far, far stranger than fiction.

So of course I saw Mr. E in Vegas. It was magical. He even had a hat monogrammed with giant lettering that read "Mr. E." And because my tour family and I were staying in a hotel on the Vegas strip shaped like a castle, you can imagine how I was drawing the obvious parallels between my story and pretty much every fairy tale I had ever read.

But what I can see now, only in hindsight, is that the real fairy-tale moment of that trip was finally completing my trip to Vegas. Almost exactly nine years prior, I had darted off a Vegas-bound airplane in a cloud of angst and fear and anxiety and humiliation and taken the first step (unknowingly, of course) toward the end of my career in television. (Read *I've Never Been to Vegas but My Luggage Has* for the full story.) What followed was the worst season of my life. I essentially had a breakdown, suffering from almost constant panic attacks and falling into a clinical depression.

And now here I was, almost a decade later, triumphantly completing that long-ago flight. Maybe I was doing it in an RV instead of an airplane, but I was doing it. I can remember sitting in the front of the RV as the bright lights of the Vegas strip came into focus, tears welling up in my eyes. Here's my Facebook status from that night:

> Fifteen minutes away from completing my trip to Vegas that I attempted almost exactly nine years ago to the day. Surreal moment. At the time it was one of the worst, most humiliating experiences of my life. But as with everything, God redeemed it in the

most beautiful, unexpected way. In a few moments both me and my luggage will be in Vegas. Thankful that we always end up right where we're meant to be, right when we're meant to be there.

The first time I set out for Vegas, when I was twenty-five, it marked the beginning of the end of my TV career. The second time I set out for Vegas, when I was thirty-five (and made it there), it marked the beginning of the end of me and Mr. E. And I know now one prepared me for the other. Everything was intertwined. The decade between two very different but very big losses in my life had given me something unshakeable—my faith. My relationship with Jesus. Certain hope to cling to when everything else in my life felt uncertain. And all of those allowed me to face the storm that was coming in my life immediately following the end of the tour.

I could fill in all the details, but the story would still end the same. So instead, I will simply tell you that Vegas did reignite something between Mr. E and me, and when I returned home to Tennessee, he asked me to be his girlfriend. We embarked upon an ill-fated relationship that lasted a mere two months until I saw that he simply wasn't capable of truly letting down the walls and letting me in, and I ended the relationship. And then . . . as we always seem to do . . . we found our way back to each other in late summer.

It was then that he broke my heart for the last time.

One day in July, I finally took a long look in his eyes and saw they were as vacant as the promises he had been making me for seven years. I saw his beautiful exterior and realized that, much like a cardboard cut-out, there wasn't a whole lot behind it. Like the mock "proposal" he had staged in NYC a few years before, he was like this great big beautifully wrapped package you opened in excitement only to discover it was empty.

YOU CAN'T LOVE EMPTY BECAUSE THERE'S NOTHING THERE TO LOVE. NOTHING THERE FOR YOUR LOVE TO STICK TO. NOTHING THERE TO LOVE YOU BACK. ARMS HOLDING YOU AND LIPS KISSING YOU MEAN NOTHING IF THE HEART ISN'T ATTACHED.

And don't get me wrong; I'm no victim here. I don't blame Mr. E for his limitations. He is who he is, commitment phobia and all, and draped in red flags. I am to blame for my choice to actively keep him in my life for seven years. I've always wanted life and love to be like a movie, and in my quest to make my life and my love life like a movie, I cast Mr. E in a role he never auditioned for. I picked the perfect person for the part too—someone who showed up and read his lines with gusto but then exited stage left without looking back. Someone who was *great* at creating big, shiny, Hollywood moments but not so great at the small, simple, ordinary moments. Someone who performed his part to perfection as long as we were on a rooftop in New York City or basking in the bright lights of the Vegas strip, but barely phoned in his lines when we struck the set and real life kicked in. That's the man I chose to act out the idea of what I thought love should look like for seven years. But here is what I've learned: just because you paint it red and call it love doesn't mean it is.

I USED TO WANT FLASHY LOVE—SHINY LOVE. NOW I KNOW THAT'S THE STUFF OF GLITTER, NOT GOLD. GIVE ME STEADFAST AND WHOLEHEARTED INSTEAD.

I guess another way to look at it is this: I used to want the Vegas version of love. Now I see that the one for me will be as quiet and unassuming as Tennessee. (Just call me Dr. Seuss.)

I had asked God at the beginning of the year to remove anything or anyone from my life that didn't belong there. And a few months prior to this final encounter with Mr. E, I wrote in my prayer journal: *God, please bring this relationship to an end definitively if it is not in your will for my life. Let there be no ambiguity. Close the door and let there be absolutely no going back this time.*

It took a trip to Vegas, a lonely two-month relationship

with Mr. E, and the heartbreak heard 'round the world to finally open my eyes. But once they were opened, as I prayed in my journal, there was absolutely no going back.

The whole point of my relationship with Mr. E was to push me closer to God. To stretch me. To grow me. To change me. To make me more into the woman God wanted me to be. And sometimes the process of becoming the person God wants you to be is painful. You will shed some tears. You might even want to turn back to yesterday when things were easier and seemed to make more sense. But if you decide to trust God and forge ahead anyway, there is indescribable reward. Because change doesn't always look and feel pretty in the moment, but the outcome of change is glorious.

Trust the beauty of your becoming and the significance of your story. Every sentence of it.

BEAUTIFUL CERTAINTY:

Sometimes in life, we dedicate entire chapters and books to people who barely give us a footnote in the story of their lives. I did it for years by trying to cast Mr. E as the romantic lead in my story, when he hadn't even auditioned for the part. And there are moments I want to take *Never Been to Vegas* and burn it page by page so I never have to see his name again. But then I come back to the fact that it doesn't matter how he viewed me or didn't view me. It matters that I took a chance. I was *brave*. I opened myself up to the idea of love, and I risked getting hurt, and I made myself vulnerable to another human being. And that is what matters to me—not how he chose to receive my heart but how I chose to put it out there.

IT DOESN'T MAKE A DIFFERENCE WHERE YOU FALL IN THE STORY OF ANYONE ELSE'S LIFE. WHAT'S IMPORTANT IS THAT YOU TELL YOUR OWN STORY BRAVELY.

So let's not regret any chapters in the book of our lives, because they mattered and they were beautiful and they prove we're bold and *alive* and willing to go out on a limb for love, even if the other person doesn't always join us there.

Prayer

Thank You, God, for putting periods on sentences I'm not strong enough to end myself.

It Should Kill You, but It Doesn't

*I*t should kill you, being told you're not loved. It should kill you, but it doesn't. It feels like it's going to.

In the silence, after words like that drop their weight onto your heart, all you can do is struggle to draw a breath and pray life will somehow magically rewind to the moment before the person you loved and trusted most in the world said them to you.

But it doesn't.

In the long, impenetrable stillness, after words like that are spoken, you stare at the one across from you in a desperate attempt to recognize a glimpse of the person you know and love. Instead, you find staring back at you the cold, removed gaze of a stranger.

What about all the laughter? All the tears? All the passion? All the joys? All the pain? All the years? All the kisses? All the history? Where is it all now? The years of pulling and pushing and forgiving and forgetting and fighting and loving? Has the story been rewritten? The pages ripped out? Who changed the ending without telling you? How could this possibly be the final scene?

"I'm not in love with you."
"I'm no longer attracted to you."
"I don't want to be with you."

Words spoken with the cold precision of a steel blade being thrust into your chest. And isn't that what each sentence like that is? A slash to your heart? Until the blood and tears run together and you're blinded by the pain and can no longer remember what it feels like to be whole?

It should kill you, but it doesn't.

Instead, it leaves you wounded. Flattened. Broken.

But alive.

Curled up in a ball on the floor, but alive. Isn't it odd how great joy and great pain both draw tears from your eyes? How love and loss both take your breath away? Such a thin line between hurt and hope. Between tragedy and triumph. Between sorrow and strength.

It should kill you, but it doesn't.

Instead, it leaves you stronger.

It's a strength you didn't know a week ago. An hour ago. Five minutes ago. You didn't ask for it. You'd gladly give it back if you could. But you can't. It's yours. An unyielding and unapologetic gift given to you by the one who also just finally, *finally* handed you the gift of closure.

Not closure by death. Closure by *life*. New life. One without him in it.

FOR EVERY CHAPTER THAT ENDS, ANOTHER BEGINS.

Your life with him is over. With the slash of his words, the invisible cord that always seemed to bind you to him is finally severed. Your heart feels vacant but at peace. And what is that flash of *something* you feel underneath all the pain? Something bordering on . . . relief?

This slashing, this cutting, this severing, this emptying, this hurting, this bleeding . . .

It should kill you, but it doesn't.

Instead, it sets you free.

EXERCISE: PRAYER OF SURRENDER

When I enter into a new relationship, whether it's a romantic relationship, a friendship, or even a business-related relationship, I say a threefold prayer:

God, please . . .

1) Guard my heart throughout the course of this relationship.
2) Show me anything I need to see about this person that I might be blinded to.
3) Remove this relationship completely if it isn't in Your will for my life.

This prayer has never steered me wrong. Sometimes it takes seven years and sometimes it takes seven minutes to work up the nerve to surrender a relationship completely to God, but every time I do, He always shows up and either strengthens the relationship or takes it away. But most of all, He molds my will to His and gives me peace to move on, with or without the other person.

I urge you to say this prayer over all the relationships in your life. It will feel scary, and risky, and uncertain, but everything in life that really matters feels that way.

REFUSE TO CLING TO ANYTHING OR ANYONE, AND INSTEAD SURRENDER YOUR RELATIONSHIPS TO GOD. THE ONLY PEOPLE WHO WILL EXIT YOUR LIFE AS A RESULT ARE THE ONES WHO DON'T BELONG THERE ANYWAY.

Beautiful Uncertainty

Lost . . . and Found

It was summer. The tour had ended. My relationship with Mr. E had ended. *I've Never Been to Vegas* wasn't completely flopping, but it wasn't exactly burning up the charts either. I had taken great, big, giant leaps of faith with God in my career and with Mr. E, and even by personally testing my own limits with public speaking and the tour. And where had that gotten me? Right back in my tiny little apartment, worried about a struggling book, missing my ragamuffin tour family. I was finally off the road but feeling strangely more lost than I had ever felt in my life.

Was I mistaken? Was writing not my calling in life after all? Why was the book that was essentially my life story not making the impact I dreamed it would? Why did I feel so confused about everything? Had God forgotten me?

This might seem like a big conclusion for me to jump to, considering that (1) God had definitely proven He was never going to forget about me, and (2) the fact that my second book wasn't completely tanking. But I had poured my blood, sweat, and tears into that book, been vulnerable in ways that terrified me, and held nothing back from my story because I truly believed that being transparent with my stumbles would prevent other people's falls. So to watch the book flounder even a little made me second-guess everything about what I felt was my calling in life. I had also failed miserably at love, which wasn't giving me a lot of confidence in myself. Combine all that with the fact that I went from walking in my purpose boldly every single day on the tour, facing fears and pushing my limits and stepping out in faith and trusting God to catch me, to toiling away in my apartment by myself day after day . . . and I was spiraling. I felt completely and totally lost. Bereft. And even a little abandoned.

What I didn't realize at that moment is that *lost* is right where God wanted me. I had made a vow at the start of the year to pursue Him above all else.

WHAT WE SOMETIMES FAIL TO SEE OR TO ADMIT TO OURSELVES IS THAT PART OF FOLLOWING GOD IS BEING WILLING TO FOLLOW HIM RIGHT INTO THE DARKNESS. INTO THE FIRE. INTO THE UNCERTAINTY.

How is faith truly *faith* if you are only willing to follow God through sunny days but never rainy nights? My stormy season was here, and I think God was sitting back waiting to see how I would respond to it.

At the beginning, I didn't respond very well.

I huddled up in my apartment in my pj's, day after day, some days hardly getting out of bed. I became addicted to reruns of *Survivor*. I must have watched five or six seasons in a row. (I'm pretty sure someone could psychoanalyze that and come up with some fascinating conclusions.) I hid from social media. I hid from my friends. I hid from God. I started to question Him a little—even after all He had brought me through that year—all the lessons He had taught me and the walls of courage He had helped me build. Instead, I was beginning to build walls of defense around my heart and my life.

Cut off from my Savior, my creativity, and the light that sharing my heart with my readers brings into my world every single day, I began to wither like a flower in need of water.

Then one night as I was saying my prayers and hearing absolutely nothing in return from God, I asked Him—*begged* Him, actually—to show up. To make Himself known. To remind me of who I was and more importantly, to remind me of who *He* is. I couldn't take the silence anymore.

Over the course of the next few days, the cloud started to lift. The sun began to peek through, slowly at first, then more with each passing day. I began to find my voice again. My fingers found my keyboard again. And as I sat there at my laptop and began to write, a little more broken but a *lot* more open, it finally hit me. I could stop trying to be perfect. I could stop beating myself up because I'm not a spotless, flawless example of what a single Christian woman *should* look like. I could stop punishing myself for not being a *New York Times* bestselling author or the world's best girlfriend or the most prolific blogger in the history of bloggers. I could start being myself again: imperfect and flawed and completely fallible as I am. Not a self-help guru, not a pastor, not a counselor. Simply me, a single woman who struggles, cries, overthinks, gets angry at God, makes wrong decisions, and chooses wrong people.

Most of all, I could stop doubting God because my life didn't look exactly the way I thought it should. And when I did doubt God, I could forgive myself for those doubts.

I REMEMBERED THAT ANYONE WHO HAS EVER CHASED AFTER GOD IN ANY REAL AND MEANINGFUL WAY HAS HAD TO WRESTLE WITH A FEW QUESTIONS AND FEARS AND UNCERTAINTIES.

Look at Thomas. Before he would believe in Jesus' resurrection, he needed to see proof—to literally put his fingers in the places where his beloved Friend was pierced. And look how gently and lovingly Jesus treated him in response. He understood Thomas's doubts and questions. He understood they came from a place of sorrow and dashed hopes. And Jesus could handle every bit of it.

GOD IS BIG ENOUGH TO HANDLE ANYTHING. OUR DOUBTS IN HIM. OUR DOUBTS IN OURSELVES. OUR FEARS. OUR QUESTIONS. OUR BEAUTIFUL UNCERTAINTIES (AND EVEN OUR NOT-SO-BEAUTIFUL ONES).

And He is patient enough to teach us the same lessons over and over again.

I was no longer where I'd been. I was not yet where I was going. I was somewhere in between—no longer the caterpillar but not yet the butterfly. I was in "the becoming," and I was starting to see that in some ways, the becoming is even better than the being. It's where the change happens. It's where the bravery happens.

It's where the magic happens.

BEAUTIFUL CERTAINTY:

You have to allow yourself to be broken sometimes without trying to cover it up, run from it, hide from it, or conceal it from the world. You have to let the pain do its thing. Allow it to wash over you, allow the tears to fall, stop asking, "How do I make it stop?" and start asking, "What did this come to teach me?" It might lead to uncomfortable realizations and difficult questions, but it will also lead to *growth*. It will lead to change. It will lead to self-discovery. And eventually, it will lead to a new and better version of you.

So don't pick yourself up off the floor just yet. Stay there. The floor has lessons to teach you. Rock bottom has lessons to teach you. This moment has lessons to teach you. Lessons that can only be learned from a place of surrender.

BECAUSE THE BEAUTIFUL THING ABOUT BEING BROKEN IS SOMETIMES YOUR EYES, ARMS, AND HEART ARE LEFT WIDE OPEN. TO SEE. TO PRAISE. TO LOVE. TO FLY.

Prayer

God, thank You for not running from my doubts and fears and weaknesses but running toward them, and for taking everything broken and turning it into something beautiful. Although I know I might stumble, I will never fall, because You hold me by my hand (Psalm 37:24).

That Time Jesus Friended Me on Facebook

*L*ate summer found me back on my quest to learn more about Jesus, which led me to the book *Beautiful Outlaw* by John Eldredge, and it completely rocked my world. It shines the light on various aspects of Jesus' character you might have never thought of before: His playfulness. His sense of humor. His radical devotion to truth. His beauty. His loving nature. His fierce intention. And it made me fall in love with Him about a million times more than I already was.

One of the things John talks about in the book is how Jesus longs to communicate and to "be Himself" with us by ministering and speaking to us on our level. He longs for our company, our friendship, our companionship. And toward the end of the book, John encourages you to ask God to show up and communicate with you in a way you'll understand. Yes, we truly get to know Jesus through reading His Word, worshipping Him, and spending time with Him in prayer.

WE CAN ALSO BE REMINDED OF HIS LIGHT AND HIS LOVE FOR US WHEN IT SHINES BRIGHTLY THROUGH A BEAUTIFUL SUNSET, A NEWBORN BABY, OR A SONG LYRIC.

He doesn't have to manifest in front of us and sit down to dinner for it to be a powerful encounter. So I decided to follow John's advice and say a simple prayer, asking God to show me a sign of His love in a way I would understand. Then I closed the book and got ready for bed.

As I always do right before I fall asleep, I grabbed my phone to check Twitter and Facebook one more time, and as I scrolled through my Facebook friend requests, one caught my eye. The person's profile picture was one of Jesus! I clicked on the profile to examine it more closely, and that's when I saw that on the cover photo, emblazoned in big lettering, was the phrase "Love of God." And all I could do was laugh. I laughed long and hard until I cried happy tears. Not five minutes before, I had asked God to reveal Himself and His love for me in a way I would understand, and He sent me this beautiful image of Jesus topped by the words "Love of God" in the form of a Facebook friend request!

Obviously, I know the friend request was not actually from God (ha ha!), but the imagery that appeared on that person's profile at that very moment, through that very friend request, was beyond coincidental.

Particularly because social media is pretty much my love language. And I had to wonder . . . how many times has God wanted to communicate His love for us in sweet, simple ways such as this, or even in big, *grand* ways, and we were too blind or busy or prideful to see?

Go ahead. He's waiting. Accept His friend request.

EXERCISE: GOD WINK

Grab a pen and a journal and spend a few minutes thinking about the "God Winks" you've experienced before (or God showing up in your life in a special and perfectly timed way). Maybe through a just-the-right-words Scripture passage, or a text message from a friend who somehow knew you needed encouragement. Now write today's date in your journal along with a prayer to God, asking Him to show up and reveal Himself to you again in a way you will recognize, in a manner that is unique and special to you. Then keep your eyes and your heart open to His presence and His voice.

The answer might not come in five minutes like mine did, but it will come. When it does, add it to the journal entry as a reminder that God longs to connect with you and that He is incapable of letting His children down. His love is our most beautiful certainty.

Beautiful Uncertainty

Finding My Way Home

A season was coming to an end. Change was in the air, and I recognized all the recent endings in my life were leading me toward a beautiful new beginning. I was ready to redesign my life once again, and since God was working on me from the inside out, I knew it was time for me to work from the outside *in*. It was time to find a new place to live, one that I loved, that inspired me, and that fit the new dimensions my life was expanding to.

I remember how frustrated I felt as I looked high and low for a new home. There were places that were too expensive, places that were too small, places that wouldn't be ready on time, places that weren't even real. There is (almost) nothing more exasperating than searching for a place to live. (Except, perhaps, finding someone to love.) But I can remember having this feeling in my gut to keep looking.

KEEP PRAYING. KEEP HOPING. KEEP HOLDING OUT NOT JUST
FOR OKAY, OR FOR EVEN BETTER, BUT FOR THE BEST.

And in the middle of that endless search, I came across a rather unassuming little ad on Craigslist. So unassuming, I almost didn't respond. It also said, "No Pets," which could have completely discouraged me from responding because everyone knows my cat Prince Hairy and I are like peas and carrots. But something in my gut told me to send the landlord an e-mail. And the rest, as they say, is history.

I went out to see the property with my parents later that very day and fell in love. There was a pond and horses and walking trails and baby ducklings waddling after their mamas as fast as their little legs could carry them. It was like walking into the pages of a Nicholas Sparks novel. It felt as though someone had wandered around inside my mind and then created what he saw. That's how magical the ranch is where I now live. I had found the physical place where my soul belonged. A place where God seemed to be around every corner. I could sense His presence all around me, in the whisper of the trees, in ripples of the pond, in the chirping of the crickets late at night as I would sit on my deck in the otherwise silent night, talking to Him.

Looking back now, it's easy to see how I could have so easily missed it had I given up or grown frustrated or settled for something less out of fear or doubt or impatience.

I say all this to make a point: I know the wait for (fill

in the blank) is frustrating and tiresome and sometimes feels hopeless and endless and like you've been forgotten. Like you'll never quite find the place or the person or the purpose that *fits*. But you *will*. Someday. And no, I can't answer when your "someday" is. I wish I could. But I do have faith that *someday* is coming. For you, and for me.

I CAN'T TELL YOU WHEN WHAT YOU'RE WAITING FOR WILL GET HERE. BUT I DO BELIEVE IT WILL GET HERE. AND WHEN IT DOES, YOU WILL THANK GOD YOU DIDN'T SETTLE FOR ANYTHING LESS.

BEAUTIFUL CERTAINTY:

The night before I moved to the ranch, I was sleeping on a bare mattress, surrounded by boxes containing every single thing I owned in this life. I started thinking about how every time the fluff and excess of life is taken away, I seem to feel closer to God. It's like in the emptiness, there's finally room for Him to move. But you know what the really cool thing is? He's there in the emptiness *and* in the fullness, in the transitional seasons and the certain ones, in the change and in the monotony. He is always there. He never changes just because our lives or surroundings or relationship statuses or addresses do. Although we are often uncertain, and our lives are even more uncertain, He never is. Isn't that a comforting thought?

Prayer

Thank You, God, for roads not taken. For detours that frustrate me yet keep me from traveling to the wrong places. For wrong turns, missed opportunities, and failures that actually protected me from settling for purposes and people and places that were never meant for me. Thank You that when I walk with You, and surrender to Your greater plan, I always end up in the right place . . . even if it takes a little longer to get there.

What If We Stopped Talking About Dancing in the Rain and Actually Danced in It?

There are lots of quotes out there about "dancing in the rain." Most of them go something like this: "Life isn't about waiting for the storm to pass. It's about dancing in the rain." This quote, and variations of it, is credited to many different people. So who knows who really said it first? I know I've quoted it and made up my own version of the quote more times than I can count. But one hot summer day I got to thinking about that quote, and I realized . . . I had never actually danced in the rain. I've encouraged other people to, but I've never done it myself. And yes, I know it's largely metaphorical, and people say it to inspire others to live life to the fullest and seize the day. But in all the talking about seizing the day, are we forgetting to actually get out there and *seize* it?

So, as fate would have it, the perfectly sunny late August sky was suddenly overtaken by clouds, and the rain came pouring down. Seized by spontaneous inspiration, I threw on some raggedy clothes and rain boots and raced outside. As I was descending the steps of my apartment, something kind of cool happened. The rain that had been pouring down in buckets suddenly calmed, and only light sprinkles fell. Determined to see my plan through, I looked up to the heavens. "Let it pour down, God," I whispered with hope in my heart. The minute the words left my mouth, the sky suddenly opened up and big, fat, giant raindrops started falling once again. It's almost as though God saw my heart and my desire to celebrate His miraculous work and wanted to honor that. I had to laugh at His rapid answer to my short, simple prayer. (Sometimes I forget that short, simple prayers are just as powerful as long, complicated ones.)

There was nothing left to do but dance.

So I did. I danced in the rain, my arms outstretched, my face turned to the sky, my hair and clothes and body soaked within minutes. I stomped in puddles and did little joyful jigs, and I reveled in the feel of the cool raindrops on my skin. It was the first time in my life I didn't run from the rain. Instead of my usual protective umbrella and frantic darting from shelter to shelter to keep from getting hit by a single raindrop, I celebrated every single drop. And it was simply magical. The horses and ranch kitties all stared at me curiously, but I didn't care. Nothing could stop my dance of delight. I was completely and totally lost in the moment. And only by actually dancing in the rain did the true meaning of "dance in the rain" finally hit me.

What if we welcomed every moment—the happy and the sad, the good and the bad, the sunny days and stormy nights—as just another part of our journey? What if we stopped fighting the down times and allowed them to prepare us for the up times?

WHAT IF WE STOPPED RUNNING FROM THE RAIN AND STARTED DANCING IN IT?

Normally, I would view a rainstorm as an inconvenience, a nuisance, a roadblock stopping me from getting to where I need to go, but what if that very rainstorm *is* where I need to go? What if there's joy to be had, right there in the muddy, slippery, stormy, uncertain trenches of life? What if instead of worrying about the rain messing up our hair and our outfit and our plans, we just surrender to the beautiful mess?

That's what it's all about, this "dancing in the rain" thing. Taking every moment of life and looking for the beauty in it. I'm starting to think the darkest, rainiest, most heartbreaking moments of life also hold some of the most precious, joyful, and beautiful moments of life. The summer I had just been through could certainly attest to that.

THE RAIN REMINDS US THAT WE'RE HUMAN. THE DARK REMINDS US OF OUR LIGHT. AND THE HEARTBREAK REMINDS US WE'RE ALIVE.

I might not dance in every rainstorm I ever experience, but you know what? I won't run from them anymore either. And I encourage you to get a little wet too. Once you've experienced the reckless abandon of opening up your arms and surrendering wholly to God and to the moment and whatever it may bring, why would you want to go back? You can't stop the rain from falling, and you can't make the sun start shining, but you can pray. You can smile. You can dance. You can sing. You can rejoice. You can surrender. And you can know you'll be okay, whatever the day and the weather may bring.

EXERCISE: DANCE IN THE RAIN

Do something completely spontaneous and child-like—something that makes your heart sing, your soul fly, and other people stare. Dance in the rain. Go sing karaoke at the top of your lungs. Ride your bike down a hill as fast as you can. Go roller-skating. Wear pajamas to the grocery store and don't apologize.

Every now and then, it's important to shake up your routine with a little whimsy and get back in touch with the innocent, childlike part of yourself that knows that with God, anything is possible. To travel back to a time when it was so much easier to simply trust and believe and find delight in the simplest of things. I know a girl who once planned a Friday night "date" with God that resulted in her laughing through a "food fight" with Him. It might sound a little crazy, but her testimony about the experience made me long for my own version of that kind of encounter with Him, one of complete abandon and unfettered joy. After all, some of His favorite people during His time on earth were children. Why shouldn't we come to Him as children and allow Him to restore those parts of us that once believed in miracles?

PART FOUR

Fall

Quiet

*I*f every season of life has a word, my word for that particular fall was *quiet*.

I had spent thirty-five years talking and analyzing and verbalizing and theorizing and chattering my days away. I had talked at other people and at God for far too long. At what point does it stop being a conversation if you never just shut up and let the other person speak? I was honestly tired of talking. Not saying I was planning to stop talking altogether. (I had no plans to become a mime.) But it felt really settled and certain in my spirit that this was the season for me to *listen*. To get quiet and listen.

I had moved to the ranch, and it was far enough out in the country to actually hear things. To hear life rather than sirens. At night it was a virtual symphony of crickets chirping and frogs croaking and the occasional neigh from one of the horses. I would sit on my deck and soak it all in and stare up at the stars, and there was nothing but *peace* as far as the eye could see.

I tiptoed across wooden floors in the silence and heard the slight creaking under my feet and was reminded of the weight of my steps. All my steps, forward and back—an important reminder and one I desperately needed, particularly in my spirit and in my heart. I had spent the past six months talking, deciding, questioning, weighing, determining, and controlling, but not nearly enough time waiting and listening. Listening for God and to God instead of running to everything and everyone else for the answers. When did I forget that He is both the question and the answer? The Alpha and the Omega? The beginning of everything I am and the end of everything I ever will be?

Yes, fall was definitely called *quiet*.

Much of the previous season of my life could have been called *sad*. I had come through a season of tears, shouts, cries, fears, laments, regrets, doubts, and very little peace. But there in the midst of the beautiful quiet, I could honestly say, "It is well with my soul." I didn't feel the need to be around a lot of people, not because I was depressed or moping or retreating *from* the world but because I was retreating *to* God. Trying to find the secret place again, where I could hear His voice and feel His presence and see His hand guiding my life. I missed that place. Something told me it was here in the quiet.

Expectation was also there in the quiet. I felt a sense of expectation of everything coming next in my life. I knew

I couldn't stay in the quiet forever. I knew there would come a moment when I would have to let the noise back in. But for a moment, for a season, I wanted to embrace it. It was where God had brought me, and it was where I wanted to be. In my cozy little loft somewhere on the edge of nowhere, He had finally gotten me to stop talking and stop running and stop asking and begging and wishing and bargaining and just *listen*. Listen to the *quiet*. Listen to the sounds of His creation. Listen to His still, small voice.

I couldn't wait to hear what He had to say.

BEAUTIFUL CERTAINTY:

You don't have to keep trying so hard to hear from Him. You don't need all the answers right now. You don't have to keep pushing and stressing and striving and sweating. You don't have to figure anything out at all, because Jesus is all knowing and all powerful and knows the way your story will go even when you can't see the next sentence, let alone the next chapter.

If you're struggling with lack of clarity in your life, I just want to encourage you to stop seeking answers and start seeking His face. Get quiet before Him and just wait. Learn to be still and to know that He is God (Psalm 46:10).

HE WILL NEVER FAIL YOU. HIS SILENCE DOES NOT MEAN HIS ABSENCE. I TRULY BELIEVE SOMETIMES HE LEAVES GIANT QUESTION MARKS IN OUR LIVES SIMPLY TO ENCOURAGE US TO LOOK FOR THE ANSWERS IN HIM.

Prayer

Thank You, God, that even when I can't see what You are doing on the surface of my life, I can always trust You are working behind the scenes on my behalf. Help me to rest in the beautiful uncertainty of not knowing what comes next, but not worrying about it because You know, and it's all good. Help me to stop striving and know that You are God.

The Real-Life Breakfast Club

As I went about redesigning my life in the fall, I had the great privilege of reconnecting with several friends from my childhood. And when I say my *childhood*, I don't mean high school or even middle school but the *way back when*. As in I've known most of them more than thirty years. There are five of us in all—two girls, three boys—and in a remarkable twist, somehow we've all managed to remain single. Me, Anetra, William, Neal, and Gene. I like to think of us as the real-life *Breakfast Club*. Gene and Neal were each my boyfriend at different points along the way. And although I'm not sure I've ever told William, I had a total crush on him in kindergarten (well, at least as much of a crush as you can have on a boy when you are still convinced all boys have cooties).

Gene was the last remaining member of the real-life *Breakfast Club* I connected with, and I hadn't seen him in at least a decade. It was great to see the man he had become. It was great to see the men and women we had all become and to see how the child versions of ourselves compared with the adult versions. I'm still a bookworm and a champion of the underdog. William is still incredibly smart and impeccably responsible. Anetra is still as feisty and independent as ever. Neal is still easygoing and quirky with an offbeat sense of humor. And Gene is still engaging and outgoing, with an infectious laugh.

We had definitely gone our separate ways in life and didn't know much about the details of each other's day-to-day lives; but in some ways, we were the keepers of each other's histories. Moments I had shared with each of them were pressed between the pages of my memory like photographs in a scrapbook, and I cherished them.

There's something special about having people you share those kinds of roots with. People who had front-row seats to your life as you were molded into the person you would eventually become—scrapes, stumbles, broken hearts, and all. Reconnecting with them was like reconnecting with different parts of myself, as if I'd been transported by a time machine or a looking glass or a yellow brick road.

With each meeting of an old friend, the picture of the *me* they knew all those years ago became a little clearer—the skinny little girl with impossibly knobby knees, a perm, and a lopsided grin. The little girl who was painfully shy, so much so that she would sometimes cry when the teacher called on her to speak in class. The little girl who never met an outcast she didn't love. The little girl who found herself by getting lost in books. The little girl who believed in magic and fairy tales and the impossible. (Yes, I suppose the more things change, the more they really do stay the same.)

IN A BEAUTIFULLY UNCERTAIN WORLD WHERE THINGS MOVE AT LIGHTNING PACE AND TURN ON A DIME, IT'S NICE TO HAVE FRIENDS LIKE THESE, MIRRORS IN YOUR LIFE WHO REFLECT BACK TO YOU THE PERSON YOU ONCE WERE—MAYBE NOT EVERY SINGLE DAY, BUT JUST OFTEN ENOUGH SO YOU NEVER FORGET.

EXERCISE: FIND YOUR OWN BREAKFAST CLUB

Make a list of people you've known for a long time but haven't connected with in years. Maybe it's your kindergarten friends or your middle school crush or your high school teacher who influenced the course of your career. Whoever it is, make a point to contact a few people on the list and even set up a coffee or lunch meeting to get together and catch up. With social media, it has never been easier to track down long-lost friends and teachers and people who helped make you *you*. During those times in your life when you feel the most lost and uncertain and can't seem to remember who you are, these are the people who can remind you.

Beautiful Uncertainty

_____

_____

_____

_____

_____

_____

_____

_____

_____

_____

_____

_____

_____

_____

_____

_____

_____

_____

_____

_____

_____

_____

_____

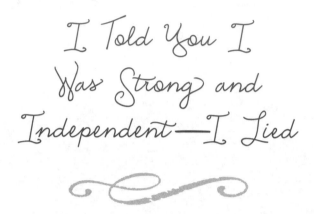

I Told You I Was Strong and Independent—I Lied

*I*t hit me one day in church. I talked regularly about how strong and independent I was as a single (and fabulous) woman . . .

. . . and yet it was all a big, gigantic lie.

The message the pastor shared that day was about singleness and how our contentment can only be found in God, not in the safety of marriage or the independence of single life. And as I sat there and let the words wash over me, I realized that although I believed I was being honest every time I tweeted or blogged or talked about how "fiercely independent" I was, I've been lying. To you and to myself.

What is she talking about? you might be asking yourselves. *Is she completely off her rocker? Or a scam artist? A liar? A hypocrite?* No. The motivation was never to lie, and the intention was always pure: to encourage people to live empowered lives by inspiring them with stories of my own hard-earned independence and strength. But the truth is: apart from God, I am *nothing*. Or in the words of Jesus: "I am the vine; you are the branches. If you remain in me and I in you, you will bear much fruit; apart from me you can do nothing" (John 15:5 NIV).

Don't get me wrong—I love the idea of being Beyoncé in all of her "Independent Women" glory. But the honest-to-goodness truth is that deep down, most days I am more Sasha Fear than Sasha Fierce. Why?

Because I can't depend on me. I can't. When I do, it's a big old mess.

I've been open about my struggles with anxiety. Although I mostly talk about it in the past tense (because I've learned to cope with it for the most part), I had a massive anxiety attack in Gatlinburg one weekend last fall. An overzealous raccoon digging in an outside trash can sent my mom and me into a tailspin. (Okay, so he wasn't a burglar. But in my defense, he was the loudest raccoon ever to walk the earth, it was 11:00 p.m., and we were women alone on top of a mountain far from civilization with no way to defend ourselves.)

Yes, I was Miss Positivity, Miss Face Your Fears, Miss Get Outside Your Comfort Zone until the minute I faced a raccoon moonlighting as a scary burglar. I spiraled into full-blown panic mode for the first time in *years*. I had completely forgotten that God was in control of even panicked mountaintop moments. (And even wild raccoons.)

So, the moral of the story is this: Even though I consider myself a fierce single woman, supporting myself, making big decisions, dealing with the flat tires of life, on the inside there are many moments when I am not so strong. I am not independent. I am weak. I am often afraid. I am completely and utterly powerless. And I suspect some of you (or a lot of you) feel the same way as me.

But here's the good news. (I know you're waiting for the good news.)

> God chose the foolish things of the world to confound the wise.—1 Corinthians 1:27 NIV
>
> My grace is sufficient for you, for my power is made perfect in weakness. Therefore I will boast all the more gladly about my weaknesses, so that Christ's power may rest on me. That is why, for Christ's sake, I delight in weaknesses, in insults, in hardships, in persecutions, in difficulties. For when I am weak, then I am strong.—2 Corinthians 12:9–10 NIV

These verses, these truths, are why I feel the need to shout my weakness and dependence from the rooftops. My very fears, inadequacy, and foolishness are what make God and His hand in my life shine so brightly. He is the reason, and the only reason, I can get up on stages in front of thousands of people, do interviews on national television in front of millions, and open up my life and my heart. I was vulnerable, real, and brave about telling my story. It's all Him. It's none of me. Yes, there are still things that terrify me and shake me and cause me to back down, but the good news is His mercies are new every single day, and what scares me to death today might be what He gives me the grace to face down and overcome tomorrow.

And the same holds true for you.

I hope you know Him, this Jesus I speak of. This Jesus I've spoken of throughout this book. I fail Him daily, and yet He still keeps giving me grace to be me. Weak, imperfect, completely dependent (on Him) me. And the truth is, as much as I have talked about "what strong women do" and how "independence is attractive" and blah blah blah, I am grateful for my weakness and my failings. They're the reason I have a message at all. They are the reason God has been able to do something meaningful with my life.

THE WEAKER WE ARE, THE STRONGER HE IS.

It's not easy being independent. Not only is it not easy, but it's also impossible . . . if you want to live a life that matters.

BEAUTIFUL CERTAINTY:

Who can relate to the struggle to show yourself grace and the tendency to beat yourself up for having a bad day, an off moment, or *not* being a strong, independent woman? After coming out on the other side of a challenging few months, I was finally able to see the greater purpose of struggle and weakness and imperfection:

> ## NOTHING MAKES A PERSON MORE SENSITIVE AND COMPASSIONATE AND FORGIVING OF THE PLIGHT OF OTHERS THAN ACTUALLY STEPPING INTO THAT PERSON'S EXPERIENCE.

I like to think that's a big reason why God came to walk among us in human form—He took part in every bit of our humanity. The loneliness. The sadness. The temptation. The discouragement. The fear. The doubt. No matter who you are or where you are in your life—married, single, children, no children, male, female—you have likely come face-to-face with depression or anxiety or uncertainty or hopelessness. Maybe you've felt like you have no purpose or no friends or no one to love you, and you've wondered who turned out the lights, and when they would get turned back on, because the darkness is scary and overwhelming and unforgiving.

I want to encourage you: If you're not okay, that's okay. If you're not always the strong one, that's okay. If you're often the weak, scared one, that's okay too. You're human. And it's really challenging to be a human sometimes. Be gracious with yourself. Be kind to yourself. Be loving to yourself. And embrace struggles and trials and fear as just another part of the human experience. God can bring you through those challenges and leave you not only stronger but also able to reach back and help pull others out of *their* struggles. But most of all, know that you are *not* alone. We have all been there at some point or another. And maybe if we can be a little kinder to ourselves, and to each other, we'll find our way back to the light a whole lot faster.

Prayer

God, I know I am a weak, imperfect vessel. Thank You for giving me courage, for holding me up, and for showing me that through You and You alone, I can be strong. And most of all, thank You for taking the brokenness of my life and making it beautiful.

A Dream Delayed, Not Denied

*O*ne quiet, unassuming day in early September, I got a phone call out of the blue that would change my perspective on the perfection of God's timing forever.

My book *I've Never Been to Vegas but My Luggage Has* had released almost six months earlier, and as you know, its performance had left me feeling disappointed and even like a bit of a failure. As much as I loved my first book, *Vegas* was much more personal and intense, and, honestly, one of the biggest and scariest and hardest and most life-changing projects I had ever undertaken. My biggest dream in life was for it to hit *The New York Times* Best Sellers list, and when that didn't happen, it broke my heart a little. Within about a month or so of its release, I had given up hope of being a NYT bestselling author. In fact, the very day I received the phone call, I had been thinking to myself: *Should I change my goals for this year? New home, new goals?* But then decided to stay true to my original goal: to seek God first above all else.

A little later that day, I got a call from my publisher telling me that *Never Been to Vegas* had just hit *The New York Times* Best Sellers list! My biggest dream had come true.

Now, I know that when we share our biggest, longest-held dreams with God, sometimes His gentle answer is "No, this is not My best for you." But other times His plan and our dreams are just on a different schedule. In this case—although I had doubted Him, questioned Him, run from Him, and felt completely frustrated by His plan over the past few months—He showed me that even in the midst of my doubts and fears and weakness and failings, He is still able to do exceedingly and abundantly more than I could ever ask or imagine (Ephesians 3:20).

Most books don't hit *The New York Times* list six months after they come out. Most of the time it either happens within a few weeks of the book's release or not at all. But I think I know why God had delayed my dream. Maybe He needed me to walk through the darkness. Through the questions. Through the self-doubt. Why? Because He needed me to reach the place where I realized that "self" had nothing to do with His plan for my life and that "self" was actually only getting in the way.

God needs us to remember how utterly and completely dependent on Him we are. He needs us to lay down our dreams and goals and plans and to surrender entirely to His.

WHEN WE FINALLY LET GO OF OUR LIVES AND HAND THEM OVER TO GOD, WE FREE HIM TO WORK THE MIRACLES WE ARE ASKING FOR.

Over the ups and downs of the past few months, I had learned that it was only when I finally stopped chasing success and started chasing Him that success found me.

A few weeks after my publisher's phone call, I stood on a stage in front of twenty thousand women at the T. D. Jakes Woman Thou Art Loosed conference in Atlanta and shared my heart. I was terrified, of course. But along for the trip with me was my Bible, the first one I received when I became a Christian fifteen years ago, and it was none other than a *Woman Thou Art Loosed Bible*. It's actually still my primary Bible to this day. Considering the journey of faith I had been on over the past year, how could I say no to such a full-circle moment?

The last time I had been at Philips Arena in Atlanta was for a New Kids on the Block concert when I was ten. Now, the night before my speech, I stood looking around the arena, just trying to picture what my ten-year-old self (swinging in the nosebleed rafters at that concert) would have said if you had told her, "You'll be on that stage twenty-five years from now." I probably would have laughed. And then passed out. Basically the same reaction I had at age thirty-five when I pictured myself on the same stage the next day. I didn't feel worthy of such a task. I didn't know why God had chosen me for it. I felt shaky and inadequate and completely out of my league. But as always, I vowed to show up and do it afraid, trusting that God would see me through it and in my immense weakness would be my strength.

He did. And He was. And although I'm not sure I would win any awards for the words I shared that day, it was an experience I will never forget. That day God and I and twenty thousand women (and thousands more via the online feed) converged for a conference that had the same name as the Bible my twenty-year-old self had clutched in her hands as she surrendered her life to God completely for the first time.

Many, many years ago, as a young girl, I dreamed of one day becoming an actress or a performer. Of entertaining the masses. That dream never came to fruition, and I had surrendered it long ago. Instead, God built up a bigger dream in its place: encouraging the masses, through His strength, and in His timing. And I was perfectly okay with that.

Oh the beautiful, beautiful uncertainty of it all. Of singleness. Of surrender. Of stepping out in faith.

BEAUTIFUL CERTAINTY:

There's so much God longs to do in your life if you will only surrender it to Him. His plan and His timing are so much better than ours. Please trust me on this one. Sometimes even your longest-held dream just isn't part of God's better-than-good plan for your life, and sometimes your dream just needs to simmer a bit longer. Or even be tweaked a little or rewritten altogether.

GOD KNOWS WHAT YOUR ARMS ARE READY TO CARRY, WHAT YOUR HEART AND MIND ARE ABLE TO HANDLE, AND WHAT YOUR LIFE HAS ROOM FOR. TRUST HIM.

Seek Him. Talk to Him. Get to know Him. Surrender to Him—not to make your dreams come true but to realize that no dream can possibly compare with the richness and sweetness of walking with Him.

Prayer

God, I know that a blessing too soon is not a blessing; it's a burden. Help me to trust in Your perfect plan and Your perfect timing. Thank You for protecting me by never bringing me anything before I'm ready for it.

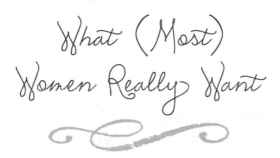

What (Most) Women Really Want

*I*n my humble opinion, it's not a big mystery.

Most women want to be pursued. Not endlessly asked to "hang out." (And especially not asked to "hang out" at 3:00 a.m.) We don't want to be treated like one of the guys. We want to be your *lady*. And we want to be treated like it. We want a little time invested into the plans. And I said time, not money. We don't care if it's dinner at Olive Garden and a Redbox rental, as long as you put a little thought and effort into it.

Please pick us up and come to the door. When you honk the horn to alert us you're there, we feel undervalued or like we're responding to a cattle call. And we aren't cattle. We're women.

Please open the car door and the door to the restaurant. Bonus points if you pull out our chair.

We want you to pay for dinner. At least the first few times. We don't feel entitled, and we won't just assume you're going to. In fact, we'll offer to pay half, but it gives our heart that extra flutter when you won't hear of it. We love to be reminded that chivalry is still very much alive.

We want to be respected. We want to laugh. We want to be flirted with. We love "good morning" and "good night" texts. (But we don't love when texts always take the place of calls or real conversation.) We like to talk on the phone late into the night, knowing we have to be up in three hours but not caring because we love talking to you *that* much. We like when you notice we got our haircut or lost five pounds. We like to be winked at. We love intelligent banter and witty sparring.

We like when you like our friends. We love when you like our family.

When you ask us how our day was, we love it when you actually listen.

We want you to have goals and dreams and ambition. You don't have to have tons of money or drive a fancy car or shower us with extravagant gifts, but we want you to be passionate and driven to achieve something that matters to you. We want to know you're willing to challenge yourself and reach for something greater. Even if you don't catch it. (We'll be there either way.)

We really love it when you come up behind us and put your arms around us when we're sad, or stressed, or having a bad day.

We want you to have your own space to grow and become and dream. We want you to respect our space to grow and become and dream too. We don't need to be with you every single second of every single day. We want there to be healthy spaces in our togetherness.

WE WANT YOU TO LOVE GOD MORE THAN YOU LOVE US.

We want you to seek Him more than you seek us. We want you to pray with us, worship next to us in church, and remind us how much God loves us when we've forgotten.

We want you to buy us little gifts just because. A single rose. A surprise Frappuccino® from Starbucks. That scarf we've been eyeballing in the window of the boutique down the street.

We want you to be our best friend, our safe haven, our calm in the storm, a shoulder to cry on, the killer of the spiders, the assembler of bookshelves when the only instructions that came with them are in Greek, the defender of our honor when we come under attack from the world or our boss or the mean person on the Internet.

We want you to love us even when we're not being very lovable (because we'll do the same for you). We want you to be willing to fight it out or talk it out or work it out instead of going to bed angry. We want you to be honest when we ask you if these pants make us look fat (okay, maybe we don't).

This is what (most) women really want.

It really is as simple . . . and as complicated . . . as that.

EXERCISE: WHAT THIS WOMAN REALLY WANTS

These are my ideas about what I hope for in a partner and what I'm sure a lot of women hope for, but what are *you* praying for in a future mate? Make your own list of hopes and wishes and wants and qualities, and then stick it in your Bible and pray over it every time you pass by it. Believe you deserve everything on that list! Be willing to be flexible without compromising your core beliefs or standards.

_____

_____

_____

_____

_____

_____

Beautiful Uncertainty?

A Lesson in Gratitude

*O*ne day in late fall, I found myself sitting in my cozy little kitchen I don't own, gazing at the turquoise carpet someone else picked out long before I arrived, and watching my cat, Prince Hairy, stalk a bug across the room to "protect his domain." (He never actually harms bugs; he just likes to monitor their every move.)

Steam rose from my Lakewood coffee mug, a gift from a church that only a year ago I never could have imagined I would one day speak at. I was eating my oatmeal from a paper bowl because I don't have a dishwasher and it saves time and my manicure not to have to wash dishes every day. I was thinking to myself how I'm thirty-five and don't own much of anything, save my precious VW convertible and a few pieces of furniture, some antique and some old hand-me-downs that would have been discarded long ago had I not rescued them from certain demise.

This wasn't where I had always pictured my life when little-girl me had imagined a far-off future complete with the grown-up version of my Barbie Dream House and my perfect Ken doll mate. And neither was this the future life

I had pictured when I was thirty and completely wrapped up in the latest hot spots and being a member of a private club and regularly rubbing elbows with the "it" crowd of Nashville. This was a life that, from an outsider's eyes, might appear banal and mundane and completely average.

But I gazed across the room and saw my giant thrift-store red chair that's so perfect for snuggling into and reading all night and my twinkly white lights strung carefully above the fireplace, and my candles and books and movies and life's passions all enveloping me like a warm hug. And overwhelming gratitude welled up in my spirit and tumbled out in the form of hot tears. And for a moment I couldn't speak and didn't want to move a muscle because I wanted to hit the pause button and stay right there in that moment of clarity and beauty and peace and thankfulness.

THE MOST PRECIOUS AND SACRED THINGS IN LIFE ARE THE MOST SIMPLE THINGS.

I've done some really cool things in my life, met some big celebrities, had access to star-studded events, and walked red carpets. Yet not one of those moments brought me the deep soul contentment I found sitting there in my glasses and pajamas in my little imperfect and yet perfectly *me* loft on that cool October day.

Look around you. Look closer at your life. The beauty and magic and wonder are all there. Only it's probably not where you expect. You're waiting for the grand moments and the pomp and the circumstance, and all the while your life is standing there waving at you in all its colorful, disjointed, simple glory. Don't miss it. Don't look past it. Happiness is here. It just arrived quietly while you were searching for it in all the noise.

BEAUTIFUL CERTAINTY:

Sometimes we get mad and frustrated when we don't find what we're looking for. Or sometimes we find what we're looking for, but it's not looking for us. But what we can't see at the time is that the things we *don't* find were never meant for us anyway.

Pause a moment and consider. . . . Maybe you haven't found that dream job yet because God knows a greater purpose you're meant to fulfill. Maybe you haven't found that perfect apartment yet because you're about to put down roots when God is trying to give you wings. And maybe you haven't found that man yet because God knows you're not ready for him. Or he's not ready for you. Or you have your eye on someone who is unworthy of you and of the gifts you bring to this world, and

God loves you too much to allow you to settle. And maybe, instead of getting upset and discouraged and frustrated about not finding what you're looking for, you can get really, really grateful instead.

BECAUSE THE ONLY TIME YOU DON'T FIND WHAT YOU'RE LOOKING FOR IS WHEN GOD HAS SOMETHING FAR BETTER WAITING FOR YOU TO DISCOVER.

You just have to be patient in His timing and secure enough in your worth to know that God wants to give His children the very best gifts.

Prayer

God, please always remind me of my blessings when I am focusing too hard on my burdens. Thank You for the embarrassment of riches You surround me with every single day, and awaken my spirit to recognize the beautiful blessings all around me. Please help me to be grateful even in times of trials and struggles and uncertainty because I know You take everything that happens—good or bad, happy or sad—and use it for my good.

One Ordinary Tuesday

I'm a big fan of Hollywood moments. Those moments, however fleeting they may be, that feel so special and so magical that you can think of nothing else to compare them to but a movie. Because I'm such a fan of these moments, I often attract them into my life without meaning to. This happened to me on a Tuesday night in October. A crazy, almost unbelievable series of events plucked me from my intended plans of the day and placed me right smack-dab in the middle of my own romantic comedy. As least that's what it felt like. I can't swear this is *exactly* how it happened, but this is how it felt for me.

I had just wrapped up my third meeting of the day at a coffee shop when I looked up and spotted him walking through the door: a guy I once had a brief flirtation with a few years ago. He waved. I waved. He made his way over to my table, and I invited him to sit down and hang for a few minutes. He accepted my invitation and went to fetch his coffee. His towering venti hot cup of coffee.

A cup of coffee that literally and unexplainably leapt from his hands as he was sitting back down at the table and flew *everywhere*. My computer and iPhone were sitting on the table, and I reached to snatch up my computer while he grabbed my phone, both of us trying to rescue my devices from the tidal wave of coffee. Coffee that somehow, inexplicably, flew all over the table, window, and floor but not at all on my clothes or on me.

As a barista ran over to mop up the mess, I inspected my phone. It had some droplets dotted here and there, but texts and e-mails still continued to flood in, so I assumed it was fine. Former Flirtation and I sat back down and had a proper catch-up for about half an hour. Only after he left and my friend Jaime called my phone did I realize this: everything about my phone was still in working order . . . except the phone itself. There was nothing but silence. We tried again and again to connect, but I could hear nothing but deafening silence. Sigh. My phone was broken.

Since I'm pretty much helpless without a phone, I knew it had to be replaced ASAP. With the rest of my workday now a wash, I made my way down the street to the phone store. Although the day had robbed me of my phone, it had been an immensely encouraging and positive day in so many other ways. So when I walked into the store, I was flying high. I was in the zone. I was excited and happy and in great spirits.

Which is why, in all my blissed-out glory, I didn't really notice right away that Phone Guy who worked at the phone store was totally adorable. I explained to him the situation with my phone and told him all about Former Flirtation ruining it with his gargantuan-size latte. He laughed and checked to see if I was eligible for an upgrade. Unfortunately, the machine came back with "Not eligible until March 1st" flashing in a rather unfriendly shade of red. "But I need a phone *now*," I explained. "I can't wait until March. What else can we do?"

Thankfully, I was able to speak with someone at Sprint and tell them the whole story of Former Flirtation desecrating my phone and, after laughing uproariously at the story, Nice Sprint Guy granted approval for the upgrade.

Great! All that was left to do was transfer my contacts and pics and other data from the old phone to the new phone. A process that should have taken maybe twenty to thirty minutes.

Instead, it ended up taking *two hours*.

"What?" my friend Anetra shrieked when I repeated the story back to her. "What did you do? Go shopping?"

Nope. I didn't.

What I did was stand there and talk to Cute Phone Guy. For two hours. For 120 minutes. For the rest of his shift at the phone store.

And it was one of the best conversations I've had with a guy in a long time. I hadn't dated at all since Mr. E broke my heart a few months prior, and it felt really nice to just have a great conversation with a (seemingly) great guy.

We talked about faith and our careers and our dreams and my crazy life, and we laughed and joked and had more fun than I've had on most first dates I've been on recently. Which I told him. After he told me it was one of the best nights he had ever had at the phone store. For those two hours, during that wrinkle in time away from work, away from the constantly buzzing phone and e-mails and deadlines and responsibilities that the phone represents, away from the world in general, it felt like I connected with another human being in a real, pure, innocent, and authentic way.

And it was nice.

And the truth is that I don't know Cute Phone Guy beyond the two hours I spent with him at the phone store. I don't know if I'll ever know him. For all I know, he had someone waiting at home for him. He did ask for my number before we parted ways, but whether or not he'd ever use it was a question I didn't have the answer to. And maybe, just maybe, I didn't need the answer. Maybe that one almost-perfect, two-hour interlude was enough. It was certainly enough to restore my hope in the possibility of meeting someone around the next corner. As a single woman, it can sometimes feel like life is a giant, confusing game of musical chairs, one where everyone around me has paired off and sat down cozily in their chairs with their significant others, and I'm left standing alone and uncertain and convinced all the good ones are gone.

That Tuesday night in October was proof they're not. That ordinary night at an ordinary phone store offered a really amazing and unexpected connection with a guy I didn't know and served as a little "God wink."

YOU REALLY CAN ON ANY GIVEN DAY, AT ANY GIVEN TIME, AT ANY GIVEN PLACE ENCOUNTER SOMEONE WHO HAS THE POTENTIAL TO CHANGE YOUR LIFE.

Or at least your night.

BEAUTIFUL CERTAINTY:

One of the most magical experiences in life must be the moment right before you like someone. Maybe it's one of those gifts single folks get paid back in dividends because God sees the other moments we're not getting to experience, at least not yet—anniversaries and first steps and inside jokes and family vacations. That moment when you're right on the verge of being completely swept up in the excitement of a new crush might be one of the best moments life has to offer. The only thing more thrilling than the newness of it all is the uncertainty.

It's actually one of those times when uncertainty feels like a gift. Every text, every phone ring, every new e-mail and Facebook message becomes rife with possibility. Could it be him? When will you see him again? *Will* you see him again? The butterflies and the daydreams and the expectation that you might be taking the first steps toward something real—it all just gives the world around you a totally different feeling. That feeling is completely unable to be identified, named, or defined. It simply *is*. And it's wonderful.

Prayer

God, thank You for sweet surprises and unexpected meetings and long conversations. When I am having a moment of sadness or doubt about my singleness, please remind me of those unique, serendipitous, first-time encounters that make single life so beautiful. Thank You that all the years of being in the wrong place at the wrong time prepared me for that moment when I will finally be in the right place at the right time. And thank You for peace and joy for the journey while I wait for that right time to come.

God's Heart for Single Women

$\mathcal{A}$s I was reading my daily devotionals one day, I came to a prayer in the book *Arms Open Wide* by Sherri Gragg that read: "Too often I have turned to you in my fear and asked: 'Oh Lord, don't you care?'"

And as I read the prayer out loud, something in me broke, and I started crying. All too vividly I remembered all the times I've cried out to God about my desire for a family and children and traditions and a tribe and people to grow old with and a husband to hold me and tell me everything is going to be okay. I remembered all the years of waiting, of enduring the space between "not yet" and "no longer," and reliving all the moments when I've felt forgotten by the God who claims to love me. I remembered the countless times of frustration and impatience and even despair as the birthdays pass and the situation seemingly grows more and more hopeless that I might ever find the simplest and most complicated of life's blessings: Someone to love. And someone to love me.

"Oh Lord, don't You care?"

And then, suddenly, in the silence of my warm and simple apartment, a still, small voice spoke clearly and directly into my soul.

"Oh, Mandy. Don't you see? It's because of how much I care that I've kept you for Myself this long."

The words washed over me like a ray of sunshine infused into my soul. My sad tears turned to happy ones, and a smile came across my face. It was one of those rare, almost impossible to attain moments where I felt myself fall gently into the hands of Jesus and be held tightly against His beating heart, a fleeting glimpse into the depth of His love for me. And all really was calm, and all really was bright.

And then, again, the voice.

"If there is never a husband, if it's always just you and Me, will you still follow Me?"

There was no pause in my spirit. No need to stop and think. Only one answer rang true, loud, and clear in my heart.

"Yes, Jesus. I will follow You."

I will trust You, and I will follow You through the waiting. The waiting. Oh, this sometimes endless and frustrating and even hopeless season of waiting. *Wait* is a word I keep hearing whispered into my spirit these days, and it's a word I'm learning to appreciate more and more because I know all good and beautiful blessings from You take time. Abraham waited twenty-five years for his promised child. Joseph waited thirteen years in slavery for his promised destiny. And You Yourself, *Jesus,* waited. You waited thirty years, mostly hidden, quiet, unassuming years, to begin the earthly ministry that would change the world forever.

I will trust You and I will follow You because I know the waiting isn't about punishment; it's about protection. It's about preparing me for the blessing instead of just launching me into it before I'm ready. It's about cultivating strength and faith and obedience to surrender to Your good and perfect plan instead of clinging to my imperfect one. It's about You loving me too fiercely to allow me to settle for anything less than the life and the mate and the destiny You have planned for me.

So, yes, I will trust You and I will follow You, Jesus, knowing that regardless of how hopeless or how dark the situation might look to my human eyes, Your perfect ones see the big picture and know the endgame.

I will follow You, *no matter what.* Over a cliff, my precious Lord.

I don't know if I'll ever be married or not, but I do know that in this moment it doesn't really matter because I have peace and joy and completeness in Him. Tomorrow I might doubt again, but His mercies are new every morning, and my weakness doesn't surprise Him or test His strength. He loves me. And He loves you.

HE KNOWS WHAT THE SINGLE PATH LOOKS LIKE BECAUSE HE WALKED IT.

And His love is big enough and fierce enough to reach every lonely, doubt-filled corner of the single woman's heart.

I don't know how I'll feel tomorrow. But I am precious to Him. *You* are precious to Him. And today, that's all that matters.

> Waiting does not diminish us, any more than waiting diminishes a pregnant mother. We are enlarged in the waiting. We, of course, don't see what is enlarging us. But the longer we wait, the larger we become, and the more joyful our expectancy. Meanwhile, the moment we get tired in the waiting, God's Spirit is right alongside helping us along. (Romans 8:23–26 THE MESSAGE)

BEAUTIFUL CERTAINTY:

It's time to bring our singleness in from the cold. It's time to forgive ourselves and our singleness and God for an infraction we and it and He never committed. It's time to start standing confidently in our singleness without apologizing for it. It is a part of who we are, and that's okay.

Our singleness has served us well. It has made us strong and independent and confident and bold and unflinching in our unwillingness to settle. It has protected us from the wrong men and forced us to take risks and taught us the value of loving our own company. It has given us the space and grace to become exactly who we are. It is a part of us, a beautiful part of us, and it's time to embrace that.

Just because we are embracing *not* being married doesn't mean we're signing up for a life in the nunnery or waving the white flag and telling God we give up on ever being married. It simply means we're making friends with this character in our story—this special, protective, unique character—who will faithfully stand by us until we no longer need her. This free-spirited, messy, fragile, often scared but sacred single version of us. You'll look back on her fondly someday, you know, remembering how she carried you through some of the most beautifully uncertain years of your life.

Prayer

God, help me to walk through the beautiful uncertainty of my singleness with peace and hope and joy, knowing Your will is better than mine, Your timing is better than mine, and whether I am single for a season or for a lifetime, You will be by my side every step of the way.

Epilogue
Endings . . . and Beginnings

*A*s I write this, almost a year later, I am preparing to leave the ranch and move to a new home. I knew when I moved here that I had found the place where my soul belonged. And I know now that it's time for me to go. It's time for a new chapter. I am finishing final edits on this book and moving at the same time. I don't believe that's a coincidence. I think God has a way of using the moments and the experiences and the happenings of our lives to gently let us know when it's time to move forward. And I step into the unknown with much more confidence than I once did.

I have no idea what is in store for me at my new place. Will I meet the love of my life there? Will I write another book there? Will I get married there? Will I become a mom there? Only time will tell.

So now I will pack up my life and trade all this beautiful certainty for beautiful uncertainty. And I know God will meet me there in the middle of the questions with the answers in His perfect timing, in His perfect way.

Because that's what He does. That's what it's all about, this single thing. This surrendering thing. This walking with Him thing.

We often reach for the "sure things" in life because they seem easier. More convenient. Less scary. But I urge you to save some room for the unexpected. Stay open to plot twists, to edits, to rewrites, to uncertainty. God moves in the uncertainty.

The wild, beautiful uncertainty.

With Gratitude

To my family: You are my best friends on the whole planet. We put the *fun* in dysfunctional! Mom, Dad, Cher, Kevin, Olivia, and Emma . . . I love you with my entire being and am so grateful for you. And to my newfound Burks clan: Gosh, how amazing is God?! It was worth waiting thirty years to get to meet all of you and call you family!

To the gift team at Thomas Nelson, including Michael Aulisio, Kristen Baird, Michelle Burke, Connie Gabbart, Jennifer Greenwalt, MacKenzie Howard, Laura Minchew, Mandy Mullinix, Stefanie Schroeder, and Hannah Zehring: Thank you for your patience and your dedication to helping make this book a reality.

To Pam Hugill: You are one of the most generous human beings I have ever met. I love you and am so blessed to know you. To the rest of the Sass, Class & Compassion Tour crew: Jaime Jamgochian, Ben McMahon, and Harold Bylar—what a long, strange, beautiful trip it was! Thank you for being my "colorful little family" for those unforgettable three and a half weeks. And a great big *thank you* to Compassion International for helping us pull the whole thing off, and for the life-giving, God-inspired, life-changing work that you do.

To my "Real Life Breakfast Club": Anetra, William, Gene, and Neal. What a pleasure it has been to have you in my life for 30+ years. Here's to many more!

To Jennifer Deshler: For your friendship, first and foremost, but also for seeing something in me that ultimately changed my career path and my life. There would be no *Beautiful Uncertainty* without you . . . or any other book for that matter!

To the ladies at Icon Media Group, Jennifer, Paige, and Shanon, aka "Charlie's Angels": *thank you*!

To Lakewood Church, Lisa Osteen-Comes, and the entire Osteen family: Thank you for believing in me and my message, for your endless hospitality, and especially for the prayers you spoke over me and my ministry. Standing on that stage in front of all those beautiful faces was one of the most unbelievable God moments of my life!

To Bishop T. D. Jakes, Mrs. Serita, Sarah Jakes Roberts, and everyone at T. D. Jakes Ministries: Thank you for sharing your platform with me so I could share my heart! Standing on the Woman Thou Art Loosed Conference stage was a dream come true!

To my friends at Project 615: Thank you for your collaboration and friendship and for the incredible work that you do to help restore and empower the homeless community of Nashville.

To my friends at Barnes and Noble and Christian Publisher's Outlet: Thank you for your support of my books. I still have to pinch myself when I see them on your shelves!

To "The Single Woman Crew": Thank you all for your endless enthusiasm, support, and love. #TheSWCrewForLife!

And last but certainly not least . . .

To my precious Jesus: Thank You for the life You have given me and the opportunity to share my heart with and to shine Your light on millions of women every day. I can't imagine why You chose me, but I'm honored to be a vessel for You, albeit a wildly imperfect one. I love You.

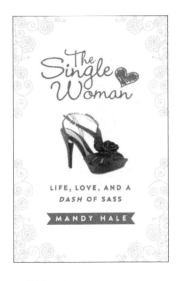